© Angela Wix

Angela A. Wix is the acquiring editor for body-mind-spirit titles at Llewellyn Worldwide. Her writing has been featured in *The Edge*, *Elephant Journal*, *The Mighty*, and *Llewellyn's Complete Book of Mindful Living*. Angela has professionally practiced massage therapy and energy medicine and continues to be a passionate student of holistic practices. Her artwork has appeared in hospitals and healing clinics as part of the Phipps Center for the Arts healing arts program. For more on her writing, art, and healing endeavors, visit www.AngelaAnn.Wix.com/arts.

LLEWELLYN'S
Little Book of
UNICORNS

Angela A. Wix is
mind-spirit ti
Her writing has been
Journal, The Mighty,
Mindful Living. Ange
massage therapy and
to be a passionate st
artwork has appeared
as part of the Phipps
program. For more c
endeavors, visit www

© Angela Wix

e acquiring editor for body-
s at Llewellyn Worldwide.
eatured in *The Edge*, *Elephant*
d *Llewellyn's Complete Book of*
has professionally practiced
aergy medicine and continues
ent of holistic practices. Her
n hospitals and healing clinics
enter for the Arts healing arts
a her writing, art, and healing
AngelaAnn.Wix.com/arts.

LLEWELLYN'S
Little Book of

UNICORNS

ANGELA A. WIX

LLEWELLYN PUBLICATIONS
WOODBURY, MINNESOTA

FIRST EDITION
First Printing, 2019

Cover cartouche by Freepik
Cover design by Shira Atakpu

Llewellyn Publications is a registered trademark of Llewellyn Worldwide Ltd.

Library of Congress Cataloging-in-Publication Data
Names: Wix, Angela A., author.
Title: Llewellyn's little book of unicorns / Angela A. Wix.
Description: FIRST EDITION. | Woodbury : Llewellyn Worldwide, Ltd., 2019. |
Series: Llewellyn's little books ; #9 | Includes bibliographical
references.
Identifiers: LCCN 2019009833 (print) | LCCN 2019017552 (ebook) | ISBN
9780738761886 (ebook) | ISBN 9780738761817 (alk. paper)
Subjects: LCSH: Dreams. | Unicorns. | Magic.
Classification: LCC BF1078 (ebook) | LCC BF1078 .W535 2019 (print) | DDC
398/.469—dc23
LC record available at https://lccn.loc.gov/2019009833

Llewellyn Worldwide Ltd. does not participate in, endorse, or have any authority or responsibility concerning private business transactions between our authors and the public.

All mail addressed to the author is forwarded, but the publisher cannot, unless specifically instructed by the author, give out an address or phone number.

Any internet references contained in this work are current at publication time, but the publisher cannot guarantee that a specific location will continue to be maintained. Please refer to the publisher's website for links to authors' websites and other sources.

Llewellyn Publications
A Division of Llewellyn Worldwide Ltd.
2143 Wooddale Drive
Woodbury, MN 55125-2989
www.llewellyn.com

Printed in China

For Amy,
who showed me from the start that unicorns are real.

And for Luke,
who provided the space where I could learn
to believe in them again.

Thank You

A portion of proceeds from the sale of this book is being donated to support animal welfare. Thank you greatly for your purchase and contribution to protecting nature's vulnerable beings. You are a true unicorn!

Disclaimer

The information in this book is not intended to be used to diagnose, treat, or prevent any condition. The author and publisher are not responsible for any damage to people or property from the use of any ideas or instruction included in this publication. We encourage you to consult a licensed medical or therapeutic professional if you have any questions about the use or efficacy of the techniques or insights in this book. Always check with a medical professional for your health concerns and conditions. References in this book are given for informational purposes alone and do not constitute an endorsement.

Contents

Exercises

Tips

Figures

"But how can it be? ... I suppose I could understand it if men had simply forgotten unicorns—or if they had changed so that they hated all unicorns now—but not to see them at all, to look at them and see something else? What do they look like to one another, then? ... If men no longer know what they are looking at, there may well be unicorns in the world yet."

~Peter S. Beagle in *The Last Unicorn*

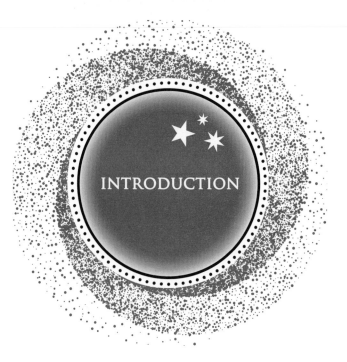

INTRODUCTION

When you think of unicorns, you might think of child fantasies, rainbows, sweetened swirls of candy fluff, and silliness. Those are good and valid things that can lead to lots of happiness, but these fabled creatures are about much more than that! And soon you'll find that out for yourself, with this compact guide to embracing the magic of unicorns.

On the surface, this is a simple book about unicorns, but at its core, it's a guide to rediscovering wonder and happiness. It's a breadcrumb trail leading you to the things that make you shine so you can get to a place of authentic joy, even in dark times. Here you'll learn what unicorns are all about as independent mythological creatures, but more significantly, you'll also learn what it means to welcome and embody unicorn energy for higher levels of everyday magic. Finding inspiration, heightened creativity, and all the things in life that leave you vibrating and make you sparkle is what this book is all about.

My mom likes to say I loved unicorns before they were cool. I've always had an interest in them, but even as a kid I kept it relatively secret. I didn't want to be perceived as childish or immature, and I felt like my quirky interest was something I needed to hide about myself in order to fit in. The irony of this is that unicorns are a symbol of standing out in all your uniqueness, and being loved for that. Even if there are haters, unicorns don't care! They're too busy being fabulous to pay any mind. Maybe this was part of my attraction to them in the first place.

As I got older and I let go of unicorns, whispers of them still remained. I can recall being at a fair when I was around twelve and putting money into a quarter pusher game. A mini-bulldozer blade moved toward and away from me; between us was a layer of quarters. My goal was to drop a quarter and try to position it so that when it landed, the bulldozer would push it into the rest of the money, causing the coins to drop. A token for a small ceramic unicorn was riding along the wave of metal, and I silently urged it on. I tried to act nonchalant about it as my friends crowded around and talked excitedly to the coins as if they would listen. "Come on!" "Oh, it's so close. Try one more." The truth is, I really wanted to win that unicorn figure, and if I'd let myself, I would have been shouting along with them. The token hovered just over the edge, taunting us. With a silent wish, in went the last quarter and ... no win. One friend hit the glass in exasperation and—*plunk*—down came the token.

I never let go of that ceramic figure. It's been tucked away in drawers and stored in boxes, but it's always remained somewhere in my presence. I now realize that it was a physical symbol of magic that spoke to my heart. Eventually, I brought it back out.

It wasn't until unicorns reemerged and gained mainstream appeal in a powerful way that I finally came back around to my love for these creatures, even prominently displaying that old figurine in my workspace. I saw that others were fascinated by them in the same way I always have been. Since you're reading this book, you're obviously one of these people as well. I'm glad to be in this unicorn tribe with you! But why are we so interested in them in the first place? I'd never been able to put my finger on what the appeal was exactly. I was never particularly fascinated with horses. So why did the addition of a single horn suddenly turn it into something that made me light up?

This book has given me the chance to address that question in a very thorough, fun, and fascinating way. It also made me realize that while I thought I'd let go of unicorns for a long period of time, they were always present in my life in a myriad of ways. My hope is that by reading this book, you too will find how they're supporting and leading you toward your inner magic.

To understand our fascination with unicorns, we first need to understand the history of how we came to know of them in the first place. In chapter 1, we'll learn about their historical significance and their various forms, and how that relates to you personally. We'll also take a look at why there's such an explosion of interest in them at the present time. Then we'll cover two forms of unicorn encounters: seeing the unicorn versus living the unicorn.

In chapters 2 and 3, you'll get the chance to understand different ways that unicorn energy tries to get your
attention. These include things like synchronicity, where
you find beauty, messages in dreams, the special "unicorn
people" in your life, and your imagination, passions, and
personal quirks. The power of color also fits in this list.
Rainbows are especially associated with the unicorn, and
for good reason. We'll explore why that is and also consider nature's material rainbow that you can hold right in
your hand in the form of crystals and stones. To cap off
chapter 3, you'll get the chance to make your very own
unicorn energy mist.

In chapter 4, we'll cover ways that you can make sure
you're awake to all the magic that's trying to get your
attention. Mindfulness practice can be a helpful support
for that purpose. Another effective strategy is removing
physical things that are making it harder for you to see the
source of what makes you shine. Sometimes our beliefs
(or lack of belief) can get in the way too. All of this will
be covered on our way to awakening our awareness.

With that newfound awareness, we'll continue on in
chapter 5 by finding what specifically makes us light up
from the inside out. We'll dive into how you can rediscover your sense of play and identify the things that set

your sparkle afire. Sometimes this can be difficult to pin down, but with a little guidance and personal investigation, you'll be able to find them in no time.

If all of this is sounding great but maybe just a little too good to be true, rest assured that you're still in the right place. Unicorns aren't shallow creatures, and we'll follow them beyond the surface level, into the depths of the darkened forest. To help support you in darker times or even bring you back out of the woods, you'll get the chance to try an energy practice for healing and letting go of what's no longer serving you.

Finally, in chapter 6, we'll cover the various steps of calling in the unicorn as part of a personal and spiritual practice. Through ritual, prayer, mantra, or affirmation, we send out our requests and help attract what we're seeking. With meditation, we learn to listen and allow for a response to our requests. And with mindfulness, we're able to receive our answer.

Listening is such an important step here. Because of this, we'll learn more about psychic senses as tools that help us receive and hear messages that are being sent our way.

Throughout this book, there are exercises for you to make use of immediately. These are included because I want you to develop a personal practice that leads you back to your own magic. Reading about something is one thing, but engaging with the material is another. Make sure you take an active role and play with these practices. It can also be helpful to keep a journal or some kind of record to track your progress. Doing so may lead to unexpected insights.

As you can see, we'll be covering a lot in a short time! I'm glad to have the opportunity to share this information and my insights with you. Some of the information in this book comes from research and various course studies, while the rest is based on my own experience and intuition. Over the last two decades, I've been an avid student of spiritual and natural energy and have studied a wide range of practices, including intuitive and psychic development, energy healing, and bodywork. For a time, I was a massage therapist and energy healing practitioner. Since then, I've supported authors through the development of nearly two hundred metaphysical and

mind-body-spirit books, and I've learned a lot from them along the way.

With that said, I'm not writing this book because I have life all figured out. Much of what I share here is a reminder of things I do to help come back into balance when the pendulum swings too far to the gloomy side of things. We are all constantly faced with challenges, and the shadow side can certainly take over at times. The goal, then, is to guide the light back in.

Shortly before I started writing this book, I was rushing through the yard and came across a butterfly slowly opening and closing its wings in rhythm. I stopped in my tracks and stared, confused at first because the butterfly was showing off all its beauty while sitting on a pile of poop. Eventually I burst out laughing. It was the best metaphor I'd ever seen or heard, and it was like it was being shouted at me:

> *This is life: one big, huge, stinking mess. Now go out into it all and look for as much beauty as you can possibly find.*

After spending so many years prior to that moment focusing on learning everything I could about the darker aspects of life (such as challenges with chronic illness), I realized that the pendulum needed to swing back into the light. I needed to find my unicorns. I needed to figure out once again what made me vibrantly happy. These are the things that inspire us to the point of making us feel like we're expanding and vibrating. They light us up and cause us to lose all sense of time.

It can be hard to find these happy things along the way on our bumpy roads because so often they're butterflies sitting on poop instead of flowers. But if we focus on finding beauty wherever it may be (even in spite of all the crap), maybe we'll be able to recognize it when we stumble upon it.

I don't have it all perfect. When people express this sentiment, sometimes they say something like, "It's not all unicorns and rainbows!" In this way, we tend to associate unicorns with an easy happiness or joy that comes unbidden, but I see it a bit differently. Legend tells us that unicorns are evasive creatures, and we all know that a rainbow is a rare sighting that usually arrives only at the end of a storm. They're the magic that we must always have our ears and eyes open for. We can lay a trail of our own glitter to lead them our way, planting seeds as we go through our days.

We can learn what beckons them into our realm and cultivate those pleasures. And we can acknowledge their presence when it graces us, whether through hard work and planning on our part or by surprise.

Even amid all the messy mess of life, we can still find wonder, beauty, and awe-inspiring moments. I hope the things I share here will support you on your way to discovering the unicorns you've come in search of.

Chapter One

THE FABLED CREATURE

To start out, we're going to look at what unicorns are all about as independent mythological creatures and how that relates to imagination versus reality. This is important to address up front because what drew you to this book may not be what attracted the next person. With clear insight into your specific interest and how that differs from other people's, you'll be able to better understand why unicorns have such broad appeal in modern times.

Why do we love them so, and how can we begin to more actively connect with their energy? What does it mean to welcome and embody unicorn energy for higher levels of everyday magic? These are exactly the kinds of questions we'll be uncovering the answers to here.

The Makings of a Unicorn

The idea of the unicorn has existed around the world for thousands of years. While we've been unable to capture them, their wondrous spell has held us captive. To better understand why they've had such a hold on us throughout time, we need to take a more detailed look at their attributes, appearance, and the ideals they represent.

The intriguing descriptions of the unicorn's appearance and characteristics are part of why they've remained ever-present in our collective consciousness. A unicorn is most popularly described as a white horse with a single spiraled horn, although nowadays the color varies and can be anything you might imagine. Historically, the European unicorn was sometimes described as having cloven hooves and a beard like a goat, with the tail of a lion. The Asian unicorn was described as being black, blue, red, white, and yellow, with a scaly coat, the body of a deer, and the tail of an ox (American Museum of Natural History). In Chinese mythology, the unicorn is known as the qilin, and the Japanese variation is called the kirin. While the indigenous peoples of central Africa were aware of a solitary creature called the okapi, it often went unseen and Europeans called it the "African unicorn," unsure of its reality. With the stripes of a zebra on its legs and hindquarters, the body of a donkey, and the head of a deer or antelope, it's certainly an intriguing mix. It's a good example of the unique hybrid quality that has characterized the unicorn in its various forms throughout the world.

As the idea of the unicorn has evolved, it has also been represented with wings like Pegasus, the divine male horse from Greek mythology. More recently, with the reboot of the television series *My Little Pony* in 2012, a winged unicorn was called an *alicorn*, and that label seems to have taken a firm hold. (Traditionally, though, an *alicorn* is the spiraled horn of a unicorn, and I use that language in this way throughout the book.)

If the variations in the unicorn's appearance weren't intriguing enough, their characteristics seal the deal. Unicorns are said to be courageous, fierce, and wild, while also being gentle, compassionate, harmonious, and full of grace, so it's easy to see why we would be curious about them. They are innocent yet hold incredible wisdom and are steady in their truth and values. They know their own beauty and power but still try to remain hidden. Elusive and mysterious, they work behind the scenes as protectors and caretakers for those who are vulnerable or hold less power than them. Unicorns are extraordinarily intuitive and self-confident beings that symbolize hope and strength and embody natural childhood magic, something that we often desire to return to. How could we *not* be drawn to them?

• EXERCISE 1 •
What Makes Up Your Unicorn?

Take a moment here to consider which animals you're most like. What aspects do you feel most connected to? Maybe it's the loyalty of the horse or the freedom of the winged bird. It could be the emotional intelligence of the elephant, the solid strength of the rhino, or the fluid balance of the narwhal. Maybe your clownish ways align with the antics of the goat or your graceful movements mimic the agility of the antelope. It could also be that you feel you're lacking in some way and certain animals speak to you as encouragement, like the lion when you feel like you could use more of its fierce courage.

Think about the symbolic nature of various animals and see which ones you identify with most. You might discover something new you hadn't considered before. Once you have your animal symbolisms in mind, pick up a pencil and try drawing a combination of them in some way to create an image of a unicorn that represents you.

Your unicorn may represent strength, self-care, independence, and more. The results of this practice will be as individual as you are, so don't limit yourself or hold back. Imagine that your unicorn is connecting with you, and allow them to express whatever it is they want to share with you most in this moment. You may be pleasantly surprised by their strength, reassured by their expressive emotion, or left a bit perplexed by their mischief. Try not to question things too much at this point. Just allow the practice to unfold with a sense of playful curiosity.

Reality vs. Imagination

Unicorns skew the line between reality and imagination. Think about what your experience with them entails. What drew you to this book? Is your attraction based in reality or imagination?

Your idea of what unicorns are may be one or more of the following:

1. The reality of an **extinct or hidden creature**

2. The use of your **imagination to entertain a fantastical beast**

3. Your experience of a **spiritual reality**, of unicorns as a high-vibration spiritual guide

4. A **metaphor** of your own search for magic in life and a belief in the very real and vibrant power you hold within your authentic self

Maybe you consider yourself to be a bit of a cryptozoologist and are seeking to discover the rumored animal in the physical world, like other sought-out creatures such as Bigfoot, the Loch Ness monster, or the Chupacabra. After all, the existence of the platypus, the Komodo dragon, and even the gorilla was viewed with great skepticism, the latter two even until the early 1900s (Animal Planet). Who knows what you might find?

In my own experience, the closest I've come to encountering unicorns in the physical realm was when I learned that narwhals were actually real. Somehow this fact escaped me until just a few years ago (yes, for real). Up until then, I'd assumed they were a parallel mythological creature, so when I learned that such an awesome animal truly exists in this world, I was completely thrown. Suddenly I felt like we all are that much closer to the unicorn since their cousin exists in our watery depths. I was overjoyed!

We touch a bit on the idea of the unicorn as an extinct or hidden creature in this chapter when we get into the details of its historical significance. The remaining items in this list (imagination, spirituality, and metaphor) are the focus of the rest of the book. Some might take that to mean that unicorns aren't *really* real but rather are an aspect of our imagination. But the idea that the things that we imagine are false or invalid simply isn't true. Our imagination is a powerful tool and can lead us to *find* truth as well as *create* it.

One of my favorite quotes comes from J. K. Rowling in *Harry Potter and the Deathly Hallows*. At the final climax of this magic-filled series, Harry is attacked and ends up in an alternate state of reality. In this space, he's greeted by his venerable teacher, Dumbledore, who imparts some wisdom that had escaped him during his life. Whether Harry is imagining this experience, is unconscious and dreaming, or is having a near-death experience in a spiritual realm is unclear to us as readers and to Harry himself. At the end of their visit, Harry asks, "Is this real? Or has this been happening inside my head?" Dumbledore

TIP 1

★ ★ ★

What Unicorns Are All About

Your idea of what unicorns are may be one or more of the following:

1. The reality of an extinct or hidden creature
2. The use of your imagination to entertain a fantastical beast
3. Your experience of a spiritual reality, of unicorns as a high-vibration spiritual guide
4. A metaphor of your own search for magic in life and a belief in the very real and vibrant power you hold within your authentic self

responds, "Of course it is happening inside your head, Harry, but why on earth should that mean that it is not real?"

The fascinating truth is that our mind creates much of our reality, and it will often believe whatever we imagine. For example, *Psychology Today* shares that weightlifters lifting hundreds of pounds activated the same brain patterns as those who only visualized lifting the weights (LeVan 2009). In fact, virtual workouts through imagination and visualization have been found to actually increase muscle strength. Talk about the power of the mind!

In our modern world, where physical, tangible things are valued above emotion, mind, or spirit, it can be difficult to appreciate or even believe the things we experience on other levels. In this book, you'll be guided to heighten your appreciation of experiences that are brought to you via your creative energy, mind, emotion, spirit, and imagination because they *are real* and have value too.

If you've come here to entertain your playful imagination, welcome! If you're more interested in finding out about your own magical nature, you'll find that as well. If spiritual practice is what you really seek, continue on. No matter which one is your particular interest, each builds on the other. Imagination creates our reality and opens us up to the spiritual experience. Spirituality feeds energy into our everyday lives. Both support our confidence to live a truly inspired life.

Significance of Unicorns Throughout Time

Whether unicorns are real or imagined, history has recorded our fascination with them. They may have first entered our consciousness as long as 39,000 years ago with *Elasmotherium sibiricum*, a mammoth-sized rhinoceros-type animal that is theorized to have had a single large horn. This "Siberian unicorn" existed in Eurasia at the same time that modern humans were emerging (Kosintsev et al., 31).

Since then, unicorns have been captured in art and literature throughout the ages, with their first depictions appearing on ancient seals in South Asia by the Indus/Harappan civilization around 2000 BCE. Unicorn legend also existed in ancient Greece more than 2,000 years ago. The first known record comes from Ctesias, a Greek physician and historian who wrote of "wild asses" in India. It's likely that the animal he was referring to was the rhinoceros, but the legend held strong. In part, he noted, "They say that whoever drinks from the horn (which they fashion into cups) is immune to seizures and the holy sickness and suffers no effects from poison" (Nichols 2008, 115).

For a time, unicorns were envisioned as fantastic beasts that were drawn to young virgin women. These chaste maidens were the only ones who could tame and capture them. Leonardo da Vinci wrote of this symbology in his notebooks around 1500 CE, saying, "The unicorn ... because of its intemperance, not knowing how to control itself before the delight it feels towards maidens, forgets its ferocity and wildness, and casting aside all fear will go up to the seated maiden and sleep in her lap, and thus the hunter takes it" (University of the Arts).

Unicorn folklore led to a coveting of their horn, known as an alicorn. This affected the survival of animals like the narwhal and the oryx, who were hunted for their horn (for a narwhal, it is actually a tooth) since it could pass for that of a unicorn. The belief in the healing power of a horn carried over to other animals and is partly why elephant tusks and rhinoceros horns continue to be poached

Unicorn folklore led to a coveting of their horn, known as an alicorn.

and sold today, to the detriment of these now endangered animals.

In sacred legend, the unicorn eventually became a religious symbol of Christ's incarnation through the Virgin Mary in Christianity. Unicorns are even mentioned in some translations of the Bible. They were also adopted as secular representations of pride and strength and as an indication of not being captured. This can be seen most notably in Scotland, where the unicorn is their national animal and was first used on their coat of arms in the twelfth century.

Modern-Day Appeal

Unicorns have appeared off and on in trends in modern times as well, especially in pop culture. In the 1980s, there was She-Ra's horse-turned-unicorn, Swift Wind. From Rainbow Brite we had Starlight, a unicorn of sorts with a star in place of a horn. And from My Little Pony there were a plethora of unicorns to choose from. Since then, we've circled back to these interests, with reboots and reimaginings. Along with this wave, unicorns have risen in popularity in our culture over the past decade, with no apparent end in sight.

Their appeal may seem simple and even trite, but when looked at more closely, it goes far beyond surface clichés. While unicorns were previously connected to the rather sexist and judgmental idealization of feminine chastity or "purity," these outdated ideas have evolved into an association with being young at heart, as well as the search for inner wisdom, empowerment, and enlightenment. The unicorn horn was once sought after and fetishized as the holy grail of healing. Now when we think of healing with the unicorns, what we're seeking is empowerment, authenticity, and personal transformation through the healing wisdom we hold within ourselves. Even seemingly irreverent humor, like the popular meme that declares, "I wish I was a unicorn so I could stab idiots with my head," gets at the idea of being able to speak with raw honesty and set strong boundaries, something that many of us struggle with.

There are so many things that have contributed to our collective fascination with unicorns. In part, we want to escape reality. Our world and everything going on in it can feel hopeless and even terrifying at times. Even when it's not, there's a steady drip of stress that can be exhausting. So we're looking for a break to recharge. Unicorns can offer light fun and joy that, for some of us, is tied to childhood nostalgia. They also inspire hope and a feeling that there are brave guardians at our back.

If you're someone who's looking for spiritual connection, unicorns can seem similar to angels and other spiritual figures (after all, a herd of unicorns is known as a "blessing") but with a more whimsical and playful feel that has less of a connection to religion and more to our grounded reality through nature. The trick is to become even more aware of their presence within the very real reality of our daily lives. That's much of what we'll be learning about throughout this book.

• EXERCISE 2 •
Tune Into the Meaning of the Unicorn

I could continue to list reasons why unicorns have become such prominent figures for us in modern times, but sometimes it's more meaningful to find what the purpose is for ourselves. What is *your* experience and sense of unicorns and what they're all about?

Take a moment in a quiet space and close your eyes. Think of the unicorn that you drew in the last exercise and the animals that came together to make it. Now think of whatever version of a unicorn is most meaningful to you, whether it's the version you drew, the popular traditional European version, or something else. Hold it in your mind and try to feel the emotional and mental connection you have to it. When you're done, write down what came to you.

The Two Forms of Unicorn Encounters: Seeing vs. Living

There are two types of unicorn encounters that we'll be discussing throughout the book. The first type is seeing the unicorn. These are moments when you come across things that stop you in your tracks and make you go "oooooooh!" They're usually things we don't come across in everyday life, like a shooting star or, as in my earlier example, a butterfly sitting on a pile of poop.

Another example is the time my friends and I were leaving a state park, content from breathing in the fresh winter air and experiencing all the sights of nature. As we started to make our way back home, we drove past an otter hanging out at the edge of a river. I'd never seen an otter in the wild before and didn't know they lived in that region. My jaw fell and I yelled, "Look! A beaver, an otter, a thing!" I was the baby blowing bubbles, so amazed at seeing a new part of the world. The otter's pleasure in the day was infectious, and we couldn't hold back the grins on our faces. Where had he been hiding? What *else* was there to see? As we drove away, I heard myself saying, "It's like we just saw a unicorn."

A sighting of the unicorn is not just seeing something that's rare to you. It's the feeling that runs through you, the sense of amazement and wonder that takes over.

Another form of unicorn encounter has to do with your own unicorn energy and the things that make you shine like glitter falling from the ceiling. In these moments, you might lose all track of time, become totally absorbed in whatever you're doing, and feel as though you could burst with happiness. In this way, you are "living the unicorn" and embodying everything it's about.

This book will help you achieve both types of unicorn encounters. Are you ready? Let's begin.

Chapter Two

TOOLS OF THE UNICORN: VISION & REFLECTION

N ow that we've covered the basic background of unicorns, we're going to start getting into the really good stuff. Here we'll look at the things that unicorns use to call out and help us raise our vibration. These unicorn tools are all about vision and reflection. When I say "vision," I mean both external (physical) and internal (spiritual) sight. And "reflection" covers the various ways that unicorn energy causes us to self-reflect and also take focused consideration of the world around us.

Mirrors, Moons, and Reflecting Ponds

Unicorns like to see beauty, especially their own. As a result, they can be spellbound by the sight of their reflection and are associated with mirrors, reflecting ponds, and the light of the moon. These symbols can present in your life in several ways. These include:

- **SELF-REFLECTION**: Casting light into shadow places and authentically seeing and acknowledging your true self

- **SYNCHRONICITY**: Experiences that are reflected back to you on repeat

- **MAGNIFIED MOMENTS**: Events that seem enhanced or distorted

Self-Reflection

Self-reflection is about self-acknowledgment and casting light into shadow places. It presents itself in both positive and negative ways. Both are beneficial when we make full use of them instead of trying to brush them aside.

Our self-reflection might come about as appreciation of our own strengths and qualities, but it might first appear as shock over seeing past our protective surface ego. When this happens, we may realize we've been acting in a way that doesn't align with who we truly are. Feelings of grief, shame, anger, and more might come up over how we've been acting toward others and ourselves. It can be confusing. Our true reflection might seem blurry and hard to put into focus.

There are ways we can move through any issues that might be holding us back from embracing our true reflection. These include talk therapy, journaling, creative expression such as art or music therapy, or reading self-help books. Other activities that we'll discuss in this book can help point us in the right direction as well, like decluttering, meditation, and finding our hidden passions. These actions help us let go of our false self and move forward. When we actively do this, it's much easier to see and honor who we truly are. We may begin to realize and appreciate our core strengths, skills, and qualities that we hadn't appreciated before.

Working with moon energy is about attending to the dark spaces and eventually lighting up the things that often remain hidden. If we venture into the dark, we can see our shadow side set against our true self. Doing this doesn't come without pain and discomfort. (Think of the folklore that says the full moon increases instances of labor.) Illuminating what we try not to know or acknowledge most of the time can be hard to do. When we're finally ready or forced to face these shadows, it can bring new opportunities to light and allow new seeds of possibility to be carried into the day.

One of my shadow places is the feeling of isolation caused by chronic illness. For a very long time I tried to sweep the "aloneness" under the rug, but eventually the time was ripe for finding a different way. I needed help to break cycles of chronic complaining and feelings of hopelessness and defeat. This wasn't easy to face and is an ongoing journey. When I finally realized I needed a different outlet, I became very depressed. Instead of feeling like I was gaining new branches of support, I just felt like I was losing connection with the people I had previously confided in. Part of my shadow side was seeing that the way I was handling my challenges was not really helping me and was also draining the ones I loved the most.

Like I mentioned before, sometimes we need assistance as we're working through the shadows. I linked to other hands that were searching for light in the dark in the same way that I was. As I sought new resources, my

TIP 2

★ ★ ★

The Different Forms of Mirrors,
Moons, and Reflecting Ponds

Mirrors, reflecting ponds, and the light of the moon
can present in your life in several ways. These include:

- *Self-Reflection:* Casting light into shadow places
  and authentically seeing and acknowledging your
  true self
- *Synchronicity:* Experiences that are reflected back
  to you on repeat
- *Magnified Moments:* Events that seem enhanced
  or distorted

sense of isolation subsided and I gained new understanding and tools to make use of.

Sometimes seeing ourselves in the reflection of someone else and being able to say, "Me too!" can reawaken hope, relief, joy, and validation that we thought was lost long ago. We can feel so alone in our lives for so many different reasons. Hope can be a hard thing to find. In our minds and maybe also in our bodies and physical spaces, we might feel very isolated. But when the moon comes around, I always imagine her saying, "Hey, I see you! No hiding now. I'm right here and I'll leave the light on so you can see you too." She hovers round and wide, pregnant with possibility, and holds back the dark. In the light we can find truth and all the things we thought we'd lost of ourselves. Secrets and lies have less space to hide when a flame is being held into the shadows.

This doesn't mean these revealing moments of self-examination are always beautiful. When the literal moon becomes unavoidable, I'm usually annoyed because I can't hide from the light and I end up sleeping less soundly. On the other hand, I also feel comforted and have a stronger sense of a cosmic guardian guiding and watching over me. When we're reminded of this feeling, it can make it easier to open up through our shadow work so that we can move on to a truer reflection of our strengths and positive qualities.

• EXERCISE 3 •
Seeing Your Reflection

Look in a mirror and really see yourself with your own eyes. Try to see yourself in this way for thirty seconds each night before you go to bed or each morning when you're getting ready for the day. This simple practice can be very challenging and emotional, especially when you first start out, so be gentle with yourself. Practice offering yourself compliments during this time. As you look into your own eyes, ask yourself what you can do for yourself for self-care. You might be surprised at the answers that come bubbling up.

Synchronicity

Synchronicity is a repetition of similar events, like déjà vu. It is meaningful coincidences that seem to be pointing you to a certain action or understanding as you go about your days. Even though the events themselves occur independently of one another, they feel intimately connected and significantly related. They are "reflecting experiences" that repeat like in a carnival mirror room—separate images that seem to be conveying the same message.

TIP 3
★ ★ ★
Trusting the Message of
Synchronistic Events

If you're hesitant to believe the message that synchronicities are trying to impart to you, write them down.
Record the day, time, and details of the events. More
events may crop up that support the original synchronistic details, providing you with further reassurance of
the message.

A memorable synchronistic event happened for me as I was contemplating potential surgery for multiple medical conditions. I'd been hoping I could kill two birds with one stone and hit everything that needed to be done in a single surgery instead of two. One doctor agreed to do this. But to receive the best treatment, I felt that I needed the expertise of two different physicians. I wasn't sure which doctor to go with first, and I also kept wondering whether I should skip one of the procedures altogether. I was afraid it wouldn't work and might even make things worse. There was no way of knowing until I tried and succeeded … or failed. It was unnerving and I couldn't make up my mind.

One morning as I pulled out of my driveway on the way to work, my mind was fixated on these looping anxious thoughts. I made my way up a hill and around a bend into the one intersection in my subdivision. In the middle of the crossroads was a bright red cardinal sitting in the road. I thought about how odd it was since the only time I ever saw cardinals in the area was on the rare occasion when one would fly quickly through the yard. Even more surprising was the fact that it didn't walk or even fly away as I drove past. It didn't look injured; it just appeared unfazed by my presence.

I drove on, winding my way through wooded roads. Just as I was climbing up the next hill, an orange-yellow bird flew in front of my windshield. It felt like slow motion. The image I saw was like a feathered sun as it seemed to hover momentarily, flapping its wings right in front of my face. I was startled but immediately started laughing.

Putting the two bird encounters together created a reassuring message that I couldn't dismiss. For months I'd felt unsettled and I was running out of time to decide what to do. Now I could see that there were indeed two birds that needed to be addressed. One surgery would align with the energy center in the body known as the first chakra, which is red and located at the base of the spine. The other would align with the second and third chakras, which are orange and yellow, located in the lower and the upper abdomen. The cardinal seemed to be saying, "Be still and wait," while the second bird came to the forefront, demanding immediate attention and action. This was indeed how things played out, and thankfully all ended well.

When synchronicity is calling to you, it's not just about coincidental events. Like we talked about before with unicorns, there is a sense of amazement when these events align. It will leave your jaw dropped, your hair raised, your emotions heightened. Your logical mind can try all day to deny it, but the energy surrounding the synchronistic events won't allow you to simply dismiss the message being delivered as just an everyday occurrence. This is magic that demands to be seen, heard, and felt. You could deny it, but in your gut you know there's something to it. If you're still hesitant to believe the message that synchronicities are trying to impart to you, write them down. Record the day, time, and details of the events. More events may crop up that support the original synchronistic details, providing you with further reassurance of the message.

Magnified Moments

Mirrors and reflections can sometimes show distorted representations of reality. When this happens in our daily lives, I call them "magnified moments." You'll notice them when time seems to slow and the event feels enhanced. This can be a large event or a seemingly very minor and mundane one. Either way, there's a sense of importance about it that's trying to get you to pay attention.

I once had this happen when my husband, Luke, was talking to me about potentially working longer days so that I could get out earlier on Fridays. "I could never do that," I responded automatically. But my response played out like a slowed video and my thoughts split. As I said "I could never do that," another part of my mind thought, "Huh, maybe I can." It might feel almost like someone outside of you is opening your mind and dropping in a counterthought for you to ponder in place of your automatic reaction. It catches on the gears, slows time, and gets you thinking.

On the surface, this example seemed like an extremely minor event. Why would unicorn energy bother with this? Maybe it was to show me that I can do things that I tell myself I can't. This is a pattern we all have. We see ourselves within certain parameters, and sometimes we need to be shown that these boundaries are self-created. On another level, though, once I changed my work schedule, I was able to more easily pursue other interests that eventually led to new opportunities. Without that initial shift, I might not have explored

> Magnified moments don't lie. They speak slowly and they speak the truth.

those interests in a way that led to positive changes and achievements.

In another instance, back when I was in middle school, I was prepping for a report on what I wanted to do as a career. This was always a question I was baffled by and stressed over from a young age. How was I supposed to know? When a classmate asked what I was going to write about, even though I hadn't realized it before that moment, I heard myself say as if in slow motion, "I want to be a book illustrator so that I can read books for a living." It was like someone else had spoken the words for me. While I didn't end up becoming an illustrator, my visual interests are what got me a foot in the door of the publishing world, and now I do in fact read books for a living. The odds of this happening baffle my mind, but magnified moments don't lie. They speak slowly and they speak the truth.

• EXERCISE 4 •
Watch for Distorted Moments

If you notice any distorted moments that come up, write them down. Note the event, what happened, what was said, who was there, and what thoughts came up in your mind as the event unfolded. Think about whether the event seemed to be calling for you to take some kind of action, and if so, what that might be. Also record any lingering questions you have about it all. Keep a record of how things unfold from there. You may end up with confirmation about why your magnified moment happened in the first place and why unicorn energy was asking you to look at and consider the details of this particular event.

Imagination

We touched on imagination in chapter 1, but we're coming back around to look at it in more detail because it's an important unicorn tool—vital, in fact. We make use of imagination to help capture the things that bring us joy in a lot of different ways. By allowing our imagination to unfold in moments of creativity, play, meditation, and exploration, we open ourselves to new potential and all of the sparkly magic that unicorns are about.

Remember that the assumption that imagination is frivolous and reveals only false things isn't a truthful rule to abide by. Instead, consider that the imagination is a powerful ability that can lead you to find truth as well as create it. It can help you build your inspired reality and connect you to your spiritual experience, leading you to your authentic self.

Our imagination is centered at the sixth (third eye) chakra, which aligns with the placement and power of the unicorn horn. Chakras are wheels of energy that exist within our subtle energy body, overlaying the physical body. They have their origin in the ancient and sacred texts known as the *Vedas*. From this Indian tradition, seven chakras are most often described, and they run down the middle of the body from head to tailbone. These include:

- **FIRST CHAKRA (ROOT)**: Color: red. Located at the hips/base of the spine. This chakra is very focused on the physical body and has to do with stability and security in the material world.

- **SECOND CHAKRA (SACRAL)**: Color: orange. Located in the abdomen below the navel. This chakra has to do with creativity, pleasure, emotional wellness, and the intuitive skill of clairempathy (psychic emotion).

- **THIRD CHAKRA (SOLAR PLEXUS)**: Color: yellow. Located in the abdomen above the navel. This chakra has to do with personal power, self-confidence, mental well-being, and the intuitive skill of clairsentience (psychic feeling).

- **FOURTH CHAKRA (HEART):** Color: green. Located at the heart. This chakra has to do with connection, compassion, love, and the intuitive skill of clairsentience, including clairempathy (psychic feeling and emotion).

- **FIFTH CHAKRA (THROAT):** Color: blue. Located at the throat/thyroid. This chakra has to do with communication and the intuitive skill of clairaudience (psychic hearing).

- **SIXTH CHAKRA (THIRD EYE):** Colors: purple/indigo. Located at the center of the forehead. This chakra has to do with visualization and the intuitive skill of clairvoyance (psychic sight).

- **SEVENTH CHAKRA (CROWN):** Colors: white/violet. Located at the top of the head. This chakra has to do with enlightenment, connecting with higher guidance, and the intuitive skill of claircognizance (psychic knowing).

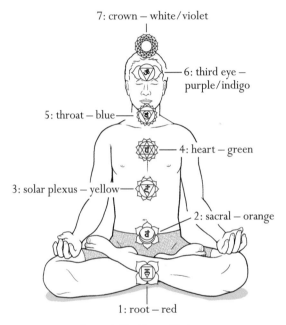

7: crown — white/violet

6: third eye — purple/indigo

5: throat — blue

4: heart — green

3: solar plexus — yellow

2: sacral — orange

1: root — red

Figure 1: The Seven Chakras

For now, we'll be focusing on the sixth chakra and the skill of intuitive sight, since this is what's active when we're using our imagination. We'll look more at the other chakras in the next chapter when we see which stone each chakra aligns with, and again in chapter 5 when we learn how to work with the chakras to clear out the energy of old blocks and wounds. We'll also learn about the rest of the intuitive abilities in more detail in chapter 6.

Try to remember how you used your imagination as a kid. Maybe you played house and pretended to cook and eat food, clean dishes, and care for baby dolls. You might have crafted clay and Play-Doh into pretend treasures or told your made-up stories through colored pictures. You might have loved making a fort in the woods or the snow and pretended it was a real house or castle. Perhaps you even had an imaginary friend. There are so many possibilities of how you made use of your imagination. As children, it's second nature to envision a new kind of reality in this way. Even when you were unaware of it, you used this ability to help you gather new information so that you could better understand the world and how to function in it.

As we get older and become more and more enmeshed in the "real world," it becomes harder to use this intuitive sight. Instead of envisioning innumerable possibilities and then embarking on creating what we imagined, we look to the world to tell us what's real. Most of the time when we're accessing imagination, it's during moments when we're being creative. If it comes up at other times, we usually end up dismissing the information that our imagination tries to bring to us. "It was *just* my imagination," we often tell ourselves. By doing this, we shrink the boundaries of our reality. In order to tune into the magic of our lives and open to all kinds of new potential, we need to stop belittling and dismissing this gift. We'll work on reawakening our use and acceptance of our imagination throughout this book in different ways, but first we'll begin by learning how to open our third eye.

• EXERCISE 5 •
Opening to Your Intuitive Sight

One way you can help reawaken your sixth chakra and become aware of your psychic sight is by practicing this zipper exercise. It's one that's often taught in beginner-level psychic development classes to learn how to open up and close down your third eye. Some people worry that "closing down" chakras is a dangerous practice, but what we're doing here doesn't equate to shutting down your energy in any kind of harmful way. We're working with our imagination to tap into our energy. This kind of activity helps us become more aware of our subtle intuition and also assists in creating healthy energy boundaries. A good time to practice this would be before bed, because you'll be closing the third eye at the end, which can help to calm the mind and prepare for sleep.

Get in a comfortable position and close your eyes. Imagine a zipper running from the top of your head down the front of your face. Picture grasping the zipper toggle and pulling it slowly down your forehead. As you do, a light shines through. This is your third-eye chakra opening up. See its shimmering purple radiance spilling out around you.

Now allow your mind to clear and pay attention to whatever imagery floats to the surface. Try not to fixate on or engage with any one image. Don't judge the imagery that comes to you. Just allow it

and observe it from the sidelines. Pay attention to the details that are being shown to you.

When you're ready to leave this space, go back to visualizing the open zipper. Grasp the toggle again, and this time imagine closing it all the way up to the top of your head. Brush away the zipper like you're sweeping your hand through a layer of sand, and see it dissolve away. Feel the difference when your third eye is closed.

When you're back in the present, write down the things you saw during your visualization practice. Every so often, maybe once a week or once a month, go back and read the things your imagination shared with you. Notice whether anything aligns with events that have unfolded in your life. Pay attention to whether you're able to more easily understand any of the imagery. Maybe there's a pattern that's becoming apparent and you can see what your imagination is trying to guide you toward.

By practicing with your third eye in this way, you're sending cues to your intuitive sight that you're receptive to these kinds of messages. Imaginative energy is reawakened. Just like working out to strengthen the body's muscles, practice with the third eye will eventually lead to increased ability.

Beauty

Beauty is an excellent way that unicorn energy calls to us. Have you ever been stopped in your tracks and had your breath taken away by something unexpected and beautiful? Maybe it was even something you thought you were prepared for, but the reality of loveliness overwhelmed you more than you imagined it would. These moments remind us of our own magnificent potential and the beautiful life we have the ability to create.

For one person, this beauty might be an unexpected waterfall at the end of a long hike. For another, it might be music by a favorite performer. However, it doesn't have to fit within the typical norm of what we define beauty to be. Yes, it's true that often art, music, and nature fit into this category. But it could also be old barnwood or junkyard materials that someone drools over, thinking of the potential for reclamation. Or it could be someone else finding beauty in complex mathematical problems. I was once caught by the composition, texture, and color created by maintenance paint over a sidewalk near a sewer hole, so much so that I took a photo of it. It hangs in my art studio for inspiration. Talk about beauty in unexpected places!

Sometimes we just can't predict where and when beauty will strike us; this is a part of unicorns calling. They appear at unexpected times and in unpredictable ways. Wherever you find beauty, soak it in. And if you hear your spirit reaching out and saying, "I need more of this," it's one breadcrumb on your path to finding what makes you light up from the inside out. Honor those requests as much as you can.

Dreams

Dreams help awaken the third eye to enlightened energy. Like I mentioned when we looked at imagination, the placement and power of the unicorn horn is in alignment with the third eye, and this chakra has a lot to do with visualization and psychic sight.

There are different forms of unicorn dreams that you might have. These include:

- Dreams featuring a unicorn as a symbolic message
- Visitation dreams from guides and guardians
- Dreams of great energetic impact
- Visitation dreams from deceased loved ones

No matter the form, a unicorn dream is rare and something to be treasured. These aren't your typical every-night kind of dreams. Their effect on you will be magnified and obvious, leaving a feeling of amazement and positivity that sticks with you for days, months, or even years.

Dreams Featuring a Unicorn as a Symbolic Message

If you dream of a unicorn and it seems to be mixed in with a more average dream, it's likely that this is a symbolic dream and not a visitation. In this case, when you're interpreting the meaning of the dream, think back to the unicorn's characteristics that we covered in chapter 1. In her book *Animal Frequency* (pages 382–383), Melissa Alvarez describes the symbolism of the unicorn by breaking it down into the following categories:

TRAITS: Unicorn symbolizes purity, innocence, faith, intuition, and enchantment. It is all that is right within the universe and is a connection to the higher realms of spirituality. It signifies the higher self, a gentle nature, a pure heart, and a loving and giving nature. Peace and inner calm, righteousness, and belief in things others may not see.

TIP 4

★ ★ ★

The Different Forms of Unicorn Dreams

There are different forms of unicorn dreams that you might have. These include:

- Dreams featuring a unicorn as a symbolic message
- Visitation dreams from guides and guardians
- Dreams of great energetic impact
- Visitation dreams from deceased loved ones

TALENTS: A connection to all that is, a giving heart, beauty, innocence, kindness, patience, perfection, positive beliefs, purity, spirituality, unity, virtue, wisdom

CHALLENGES: Being ditzy, being naïve, flighty, impractical expectations, tendency to live in a fantasy world

ELEMENT(S): Earth, water

PRIMARY COLOR(S): White

APPEARANCES: Unicorns often appear when it's time to connect to your core essence, inner being, and higher self. It can mean your spirit guides are trying to reach you, but you're not listening. When you see a unicorn, stop what you're doing and listen telepathically for unique messages. It means to believe in yourself and have faith that everything will work out how the universe intends. Connecting with a 1unicorn means to delve into your own exceptional creativity and to open yourself to the enchanting ways of the mystical realms, to believe in your intuition and psychic abilities. It means it's time to experience spiritual growth and to discover the mysteries of the universe. You are pure of heart and connected to the divine.

ASSISTS WHEN: You are experiencing spiritual growth, are working on developing your intuition or psychic abilities, are connecting with your spirit guides, and are searching for the meaning of your life. Unicorn helps you learn patience and to have faith in that which you cannot see. If you've been feeling out of sorts or stressed out, unicorn helps you to see the miracles in your life. If you've lost touch with the beauty of your relationship with the world around you, unicorn helps you see with a sense of wonder and awe. If you feel burdened with too much responsibility, or are feeling depressed or anxious, unicorn helps to clear away the negativity, release judgmental tendencies, and replace these with a positive lightness of being. Unicorn can travel throughout the universe, so it can guide you during your own travels. Seeing unicorn means to trust in your instincts and soul essence, your true nature. Unicorn allows you to see purity and beauty in everything.

FREQUENCY: Unicorn's frequency is magical like the tinkling sound of chimes or small high-pitched bells. It is light and airy and flows like a gentle breeze. It is reflective like the light of the moon and when connected to your frequency can inspire and raise you to even higher frequencies.

When interpreting unicorn dream symbolism, you might also consider the specific appearance of how the unicorn showed itself to you. Did it have the steady strength of a broad horse? Or did it present with the litheness of a graceful gazelle? Maybe wisdom or knowledge was symbolized by its beard/goatee. If the unicorn was slight of stature, this may be a sign that you can hold power, even in a delicate state. Pay attention to its specific physical characteristics, and think about what it might be saying in terms of qualities and strengths that it's encouraging you to embrace in this moment of your life.

Visitation Dreams from Guides and Guardians

It may be that your dream is actually a true visitation from a unicorn who is acting as a guide. Visitation dreams have an air of significance. Strong positive emotion and energy remains with you long after these dreams, almost as though you've been cocooned in buoyancy for a time.

When a spirit guide or guardian comes to you in a dream (whether in unicorn form or not), it's a strong sign that you're in a phase of growth and transition. If you've been asking for confirmation of the presence of your guide, this is their response.

How can you be certain that this is a true visitation and not just a regular dream of your mind processing your day or coming up with random stories? I can always tell a visitation dream from an average one because when it's a true visitation, I usually wake up within the dream. I might not become fully lucid, but I'll at least begin to question whether or not I am actually awake or am dreaming. This has happened enough times that I've been able to be a more active participant in the dream.

It can be a challenge not to wake up when you realize you're dreaming. If you find yourself experiencing this kind of thing, something you can do to stabilize the dream is to focus on a certain detail of an item around you in the dream. Once you're comfortable with the fact that you're dreaming, you can try to consciously interact with your guides. The more that lucid dreaming occurs for you, the better you'll get at it, but for me it remains a rare occurrence that highlights the importance of a dream.

Even if lucidity is not part of your experience, these types of visitation dreams still impart a great deal of love, affection, nurturing, protection, and intimate connection. If you feel incredibly safe and as though your energy is becoming expansive, these are all signs of a visitation. Even if you can't remember the specifics of the dream, you may also awaken feeling as though you've gained newfound wisdom. If you feel like you were given valuable wisdom that you can no longer recall, don't worry. It just means that your guide or guardian shared it with you on a level that's hard to access consciously. It's still there and you're still making use of it.

• EXERCISE 6 •
Meditation after a Visitation Dream

Don't worry if lucid dreaming isn't something that you experience during a visitation dream. I consider it to be a bonus, not a necessity. There's still a great deal that you can get out of visitation dreams, even if you can only consciously consider them after you've awakened. Once you're awake, go through all the details of what occurred in the dream, who appeared, what it felt like, etc. If you want to consciously commune with this guide further, you can go into a meditation as a follow-up practice.

Envision the same scene you were in during your dream and then see how things unfold from there within the meditation while you are awake.

Dreams of Great Energetic Impact

A unicorn may appear as your guide in a visitation dream, but instead of seeing a defined figure, it's more likely you'll have a dream that allows you to experience a heightened connection to energy and love. These dreams will leave you with a sense of amazement because you're so immersed in the details: the feel, sights, sounds, smells, tastes. Colors in these dreams are vibrant. Energy is something you can easily see and understand. It's an experience that leaves a strong imprint, sometimes even years later.

Instead of seeing a unicorn figure, you're brought into an environment that explores all the magic they represent. You might have a dream that gives you a peek at another realm or shows you how you can move energy and connect easily with plants, animals, other people, and even those in spirit.

In one such dream, I had died and wanted to comfort my husband and let him know that I was still there, but he wasn't able to hear me as a spirit. A fox came to me and allowed my spirit to merge into his physical body as a way to get my husband to hear me. I ran through the woods as the fox and eventually jumped into a deer, a rabbit, a frog, and even a drop of water that rolled along the edge of a pond. Just before the drop merged into the greater body of water, I awoke. My own fear of losing myself if I became one with the larger body of energy caused me to wake up, but I always wonder what I would have experienced if I'd let myself continue. The small portion of the dream that I did get to experience left me amazed at the sense of connection I felt from the morphing experience and the loving offering of assistance from so many different beings.

Visitation Dreams from Deceased Loved Ones

This category is different from the others because it's not about unicorns specifically. You might dream of a unicorn that is symbolic, connect with its impressive energy, or receive a visitation from your unicorn guide or other guardians. These dreams have more obvious unicorn associations. I also consider visitation dreams from loved ones to be unicorn dreams because true visitations are rare and you never know when or to whom the loved one is going to appear.

When a loved one passes away, those who are left behind often hope for a visitation in some form. Yet for whatever reason, these visitation dreams frequently end up being imparted to those who are outside of the immediate circle. So instead of a father, mother, or sibling being on the receiving end, the visitation is experienced by a friend or coworker, who then might relay it to the core family. I believe this is due to the fact that those who most immediately share life experience and familial energy with the deceased person are too blocked from grief to make a clear connection. Even in normal circumstances, our physical energy resonates at a denser vibration than spirit. For communication to come through, often we have to meet in the middle, with spirit lowering their energy while we raise ours. (Psychic mediums connect with those who've passed on and are skilled at raising their energy so that it's easier for spirit communication to occur.) When we're in the throes of grief, our energy becomes even

I also consider visitation dreams from loved ones to be unicorn dreams because true visitations are rare.

lower. Before direct communication can occur, we need time to heal.

This happened after my older sister, Amy, died. In life we had been so connected, especially when it came to spiritual and psychic interests. She was a yoga instructor and I a massage therapist, and we were both intrigued by alternative and energetic therapies. We would sometimes practice our intuitive abilities together and always knew when the other was about to call. So if a visitation came from her, I'd hoped and assumed it would be to me.

Instead, we heard of visitations that came to others. I had plenty of dreams where Amy appeared, but they were odd, confusing, and dark. Instead of visitations, these were dreams of my mind trying to process her death and my grief. Eventually, as time began to heal the pain, visitation dreams from Amy did come to me. These kinds of dreams share the beautiful intensity of dreams of great energetic impact and the lucidity of visitations from guides and guardians. Often, visitations from deceased loved ones impart a sense of community and share a continued storyline of how your loved one is doing and what they've been up to.

In one such dream, Amy was at a sunny outdoor family gathering with other deceased family members, and I was invited just long enough to receive a hug from her and a glimpse of the festivities from a distance. Her hug is always a moment within these visitation dreams when I become very lucid. In another visitation, I was in a school theater filled with people and Amy was sitting next to me. I was very aware of the fact that she had passed, which is also something that causes me to become lucid within these dreams. I noticed that she was breathing and thought, "She shouldn't need to breathe anymore. They must do that to seem more normal and not freak us out."

I wondered what Amy had been up to since her passing, and in response to that thought, I saw a door with a doodled heart on it. (Amy always signed her name with this styled heart, and it became a symbol of her for our family.) Amy was "opening the door" for people to walk through, helping others achieve their dreams with philanthropy and creative endeavors. In the theater, the screen lit up and the words that appeared on it read, "Thank you, Amy." There was a swelling sense of pride that washed over the space, and I realized that everyone was gathered there to celebrate and thank her for the achievements she'd made in helping others during her time in spirit.

There's nothing quite like a visitation dream. Thinking of this last one still makes me tear up every time. If you have lost someone you love, I hope the unicorn blesses you with its presence to help soothe and heal your loss.

How to Prepare, Ask For, and Record Your Unicorn Dreams

For the most part, unicorn dreams follow their own agenda. Unicorns are elusive until they decide to make themselves known. They flit in, leave us in awe, and then disappear until the magical moment they decide to return again. While there's usually an unknown timing to their appearance, there are things we can do to encourage their visits. This is especially the case for visitation dreams of guides and guardians. Becoming regularly aware of your dreams makes it much more likely that you'll catch unicorn dreams when they arrive. Instead of brushing them off or forgetting them entirely, you'll be ready to catch them.

PREPARATION: Keep paper and a writing utensil by your bed so you can easily write down your dreams when you wake up. Set up your sleeping space so it's calming to you. Don't have a TV or cell phone in the space. Eliminate blue lights and electromagnetic frequencies as much as possible, since these disturb our natural sleep patterns and can hinder our ability to get into the deeper levels of sleep where we dream. Keep the space cool if you can. Sometimes adding weight, like extra comforters or a weighted blanket, can help you relax and sleep better. Do something that relaxes you before bed, like reading or journaling, to get the cluttered thoughts of the day out of your mind. Don't eat within two hours of bedtime if you can help it, as having an active stomach can disrupt your quality of sleep.

ASK FOR A UNICORN DREAM: Whether the dream ends up being symbolic, energetic, or a form of visitation, you can encourage the appearance of a unicorn dream by asking for one. Before you go to sleep, say out loud or in your mind, "I am open to experiencing a unicorn dream."

JOURNAL YOUR DREAMS: This doesn't have to be an in-depth description. Just jotting down a line or two each morning from whatever you can remember of your dreams is enough to cue your mind to the fact that it should be helping you remember these messages when they arrive. When you receive an obvious unicorn dream, go into more detail when you record it. Write down what you saw, who else was present, and whatever seemed to be the heart of the message that was being imparted. If no words were spoken, then pay attention to the imagery and emotions that were involved. For example, whether the environment was calm and peaceful or vibrantly alive with energy can guide you to what it was trying to tell you. Take a crack at interpreting what the various dream images symbolized as well.

Passions

When we're on the lookout for how we can make our lives glitter and glow, attending to our passions should be high on the list. When we find the activities, actions, people, and places that make us feel *alive* and purposeful, we are that much closer to living the unicorn dream. Our passions can heighten our senses, leave us lost in time, bring pleasure, and impart a feeling of purpose. They energize and motivate us.

As an extreme procrastinator, I know that a very authentic passion will smash that hesitating tendency to bits. Breaking down personal barriers is one thing, but passions tend to break down outer obstacles as well. The drive that comes to back up a passion often finds a way to push through to the other side of challenges, even for something that might initially seem insurmountable.

That all sounds pretty great, but it's not very helpful if you don't know what your passions are to begin with. It's not always a given that we know. For some people, their passion is an obvious talent or skill, but possessing a certain ability doesn't always mean that's our true passion. So how do we discover what our true passions are? To figure it out, ask yourself these questions:

- What inspires you?
- Where do you lose track of time and feel your energy expanding?
- What are you already doing and tinkering around with that you enjoy?
- What comes to you without effort?
- What feels as though it is asking to be expressed?

Playfulness is the map to our simple pleasures. Those pleasures are the breadcrumbs leading us to what our true passions are. For example, in the movie *P.S. I Love You*, the main character, Holly, loves shoes. Her closet is stuffed with them, and it seems this is the one luxury she allows herself, although she makes it very clear she's only able to indulge because she buys them from eBay. Even though she's living on a budget, she finds a way to access something that she really enjoys. When Holly is searching for her calling, she stumbles upon the realization that designing shoes is her passion in life, although up until that point she never could have imagined it.

The point here is that our passion is usually staring us right in the face, hidden in plain sight. Look at what you're already having fun with. Even if it's not something you're acting on yet in a passion-driven way, it could be the seed of potential you've been looking for.

When she was still in the midst of her search, Holly said, "All I know is, if you don't figure out the 'something,' you'll just stay ordinary. And it doesn't matter if it's a work of art or a taco or a pair of socks. Just create something new and there it is, and it's you, out in the world, outside of you. And you can look at it or hear it, or read it, or feel it, and you know a little bit more about you. A little bit more than anybody else does" (LaGravenese and Rogers 2007).

TIP 5

★ ★ ★

Discovering Your True Passions

So how do you discover what your true passions are?
To figure it out, ask yourself these questions:

- What inspires you?
- Where do you lose track of time and feel your energy expanding?
- What are you already doing and tinkering around with that you enjoy?
- What comes to you without effort?
- What feels as though it is asking to be expressed?

When Holly says you'll stay "ordinary," I take this to mean that if you don't make the effort to identify and act on your passions, however big or small they may be, you will lose out on really knowing yourself. You will miss out on being able to know your extra-ordinary self and truly shine.

Your passions don't have to be extravagant things. You don't need to be a perfect pianist or the best chef in the world. Plunking around on the piano can be just as strong a passion, even if it sounds a bit terrible. If you adore baking but don't see it as your life's calling, that's okay. It can still be a passion. The test is in how happy it makes you.

Part of what clarified my own passions was looking at the things I pinned on Pinterest or was drawn to on Instagram. From there, I could see what images captivated me most, where I find beauty, and what words sucked me in. This helped me realize a minor passion for shabby interior design and a very large passion for textile art and poetry. These were things I'd dabbled in for a long time but hadn't felt confident enough in to make my own.

Once I saw the true passion though, I fully acknowledged and acted on it. Watching for cheap vintage things that I could repurpose became a really fun hobby, and little by little my home space transformed into the shabby chic style I love. I let go of other creative outlets I'd attempted over the years and focused on my textile hoop art with embroidery, weaving, and painting. And I promised myself that I'd write at least one poem every day for a month, which led to a more steady writing habit that continued long after. When I made these passions something I was watchful for and active about, their everyday presence led to a natural uptick in happiness.

Unicorns are passionate about themselves and the happiness of the creatures around them. When we feed our own passions and light ourselves up, we light up those around us along the way.

Personal Quirks

In a similar way to how you are looking for your passions, also look at the things that make up your personal quirks. Don't get caught up on the word *quirks* though. I don't mean broken or dysfunctional. The kind of quirks that unicorn energy makes use of are the things about you that set you apart and make you interesting and unique. Often these are the exact things we try to hide from society and even those who are closest to us, at least until we build enough self-confidence with being ourselves. This is because our interests or actions may not be well understood or accepted by others and may be judged as weird or odd. As a survival instinct, many of us end up trying to bury our uniqueness as much as we possibly can in an attempt to simply blend in.

The reason it's important to look for and embrace the things that make you different is because unicorn energy flows through what makes you *you*. Your quirks are there for a reason. Just like with our passions, when we light up our quirky selves, we inspire others to do the same. How much better would the world be if we could all be our true interesting selves?

You can try to embrace the magic of your passions and everything that makes you joyful, but fully integrating all of your hidden quirks puts the missing puzzle piece into place. It makes things click and acts as a kind of power enhancement because you're no longer denying who you are. Instead of always trying to find and seek out the sparkle moments in your external life, you embody that energy and find it sprinkling out of you as you move about your days.

Another reason it's so important to look at our quirks is because they're often tied very closely to our passions.

Looking for your quirks can be yet another thing that helps you figure out what your passions are.

Think about the unexpected or unconventional things about yourself that you can embrace. Maybe your passion drives your quirkiness; if it's some obscure thing that no one else around you does, that could be it. Maybe you keep Christmas decorations up all year round because they make you really happy. Maybe you have a collection of something that others might find odd but you absolutely love. Or perhaps you're drawn to a unique hobby or niche interest that most people don't have a lot of knowledge about. Here in my home state of Wisconsin, there's a competition where participants try to do their best impersonation of a cow. It's something enough people are enthusiastic about doing that it's become an event. Who knew?

One of my quirks growing up was an avid interest in metaphysics. Spirit communication, psychic ability, and energy therapies were all *fascinating* to me. This was before New Age material became more mainstream, so it was something I hid from most people. It wasn't until I connected with others who I knew shared the same interests that I became more open about it.

I find my interest in this material to be less of a quirk now because I've embraced it to the point that it plays a role in my everyday life. It's just a part of who I am. I talk to spirits. I practice energy work. I actively use my psychic abilities, so much so that my husband often exclaims with a laugh, "Get out of my head!" when I've heard his thoughts before he's had a chance to say them out loud. But for people who don't know these things about me or who don't have these similar interests, finding this out about me can definitely seem unusual.

Think about the things that make you who you are. Think especially about the things that you tend to try to hide from people. Consider the reasons why you feel you can't share all of who you are with others. Don't judge it; it's fine if you feel that you need to keep some of your quirks to yourself for now. Even if that's the case, there are still ways you can nurture them. Finding library books, an online group, or an in-person class you can take to connect with others who have the same unique interests could all be good places to start.

Your Unicorn People

The final unicorn tool we'll be looking at in this chapter is our unicorn people. Animals, especially significant pets, can also fall in this category, but for simplicity's sake I'll be calling them "people" too. Unicorn people come in two types:

- **LONG-LASTING UNICORNS:** People who inspire and nurture you
- **SHORT-BURST UNICORNS:** People who dip in and out of your life in moments of need, offering acts of kindness at just the right time

Long-Lasting Unicorns: People Who Inspire and Support You

Long-lasting doesn't necessarily mean these individuals are a part of your life for years or decades. They may have been your teacher for a year or even a short-term sub. But they were with you long enough to make a lasting impact that helped to inspire and nurture you in some way. It's likely that they were someone who took an interest in your well-being. However, they might also be someone you've never actually met. Perhaps they're someone you heard about and something about them stayed with you in a meaningful way.

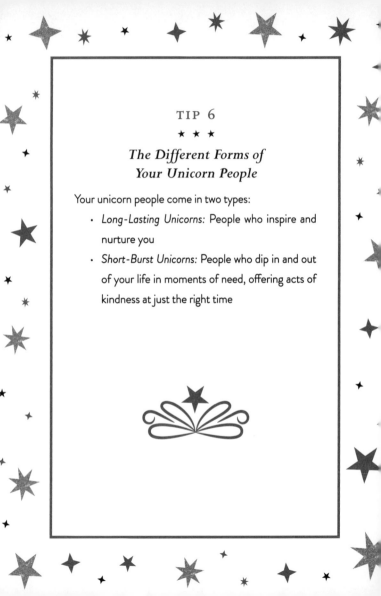

TIP 6

★ ★ ★

The Different Forms of
Your Unicorn People

Your unicorn people come in two types:

- *Long-Lasting Unicorns:* People who inspire and nurture you
- *Short-Burst Unicorns:* People who dip in and out of your life in moments of need, offering acts of kindness at just the right time

Some of my long-lasting unicorns include a grandparent, a great-uncle, a few select teachers, an artist, and a dog. When I think of these individuals, there is something specific to each of them that I've carried with me, sometimes literally. In an elementary school class, we painted stones into ladybugs, and I currently have mine on my work desk. I've somehow carried it with me over several decades now, from my original home to college, apartments, and a couple houses. It's a symbol of a nurturing teacher and the creative inspiration I felt during my time with her.

There can be lots of different reasons why we might consider someone to be one of our unicorn people. It could be a sense of unconditional love they provide or encouragement for the development of our passions. Maybe they've inspired the direction of our goals and aspirations, or perhaps they've provided an example for who we want to be.

Artist Frida Kahlo is someone who's been an inspiration to me for various reasons, even though she lived before my time. Some of this comes from her creativity. She also had a confidence that I admire, dressing her hair with flowers and adorning herself almost to the level of costume for the love of it. She didn't seem to care what others might think, while I'm someone who tends to care far too much. At times I've let this hold me back and have definitely tried to blend in and go unnoticed. Frida reminds me to express my true self without apology. I need to stand up and sing, pick up a brush and paint in my own unique way, write the things that are asking to spill out of me, and share my creativity with others. This isn't a recipe for blending in, and Frida has become my inspiration to stand in all my unique and creative beauty.

Additionally, Frida and my Great-Uncle Stanley are both individuals who lived with chronic conditions. Even with the difficulties they faced, they still lived vibrantly. While we all face challenges, I find a high level of inspiration in these two people because their shadow experiences of dealing with longtime health conditions are something I can intimately relate to.

I find strength in the memory of Stanley's grand smile that shone like sunshine and lit up my heart. As a young child, I never really considered his paralyzed state to be something that challenged him. In fact, it became just another piece of his playfulness. He'd sit Amy and me on his lap and drive us around on his electric wheelchair, laughing right along with us. Frida found respite in her painting and achieved her dreams despite great pain and confinement. They both give me faith that despite the burden, I can do it too.

• EXERCISE 7 •
Find Your Unicorn People

Think of who your unicorn people are. These will be those who have helped you work through your challenges. Who do you look up to and find inspiration in? At first it might be difficult to think of who these individuals are. For some reason, I had a huge mental block around this. (We *are* searching for unicorns after all.) It wasn't until I spent time meditating on it that I was finally able to identify who these individuals are for me.

Take a quiet moment and ponder your life challenges, obstacles, goals, and inspirations. Feel the emotions that come up for you and follow them. Think about the people who have soothed your pain or helped you find solutions to your problems or those who have consistently supported your dreams, even in subtle ways. Your memories might take you back to a certain age or moment in time. Sit in the moment and feel the space.

Pay attention to whether there is anyone else in this space with you. If there is, they may be someone who had significance during that phase of your life. Multiple memories might surface that are trying to show you a pattern. Each memory might reveal a similar feeling or issue that your unicorn person has helped you with. Again, try to pay attention to the emotions that come with it. Just like when you're trying to think of something and it's on the tip of your tongue, you might tune into the feeling and see if that leads you to whatever it is you are trying to recall. Our emotions can be a very helpful guide in this way.

You can also look to the things you've carried with you in your environment. Like my painted ladybug rock, you likely have something that, for whatever reason, you've chosen to keep with you over the years. Think of who else was connected to this item. Were they significant to you in some way?

If you're still having a hard time thinking of who your unicorn people are, don't worry. They might be so "everyday" present to you that you don't even realize they are so significant. Many of mine came as a surprise. I didn't recognize them right away, but they kept tapping on my door and rising to the surface in my thoughts. This happened with such regularity that eventually I realized their significance. You've opened the door for the answer to eventually come to you. Return to this exercise every so often and see if new information is waiting to be known.

★ ★ ★

Clarifying who our unicorn people are helps us in several ways. First, we can acknowledge and honor the good energy they've provided to us. It's a bit like the question "If a tree falls in the forest and no one hears it, does it make a sound?" If you don't acknowledge that someone made a difference in your life, it's harder to recognize the impact they made. Your acknowledgment sends a message to yourself that *yes,* this really happened, and *yes,* it made a difference in your life.

With this acknowledgment, it then becomes easier to realize the various ways your unicorn people have influenced you. And from those influences you can sometimes glean even more information about your needs, values, passions, and goals. Acknowledging the influence of others becomes a mirror by which you begin to more clearly see your authentic unicorn self as well.

When a Unicorn Turns Out to Be a Rhino

We also need to be aware that sometimes our inspirations fall short when we come face to face with what they truly are. Seeing behind a false representation that we thought was authentic can be really disheartening. It can lead to feelings of anger, betrayal, and even grief over the loss of something we found support and inspiration from. We thought we knew someone. We were inspired and energized by what they represented to us. When we realize that our vision wasn't accurate, the feeling of disappointment and disillusionment can be harsh.

These moments can be a call to find the hero-self. We often look for what we need *outside* of ourselves. Here we're reminded to look *within* and be our own hero instead.

• EXERCISE 8 •
Acknowledging the Unicorn
and the Rhino

Think of the people you've looked up to in your life. Write down those who have proven to be a true unicorn for you, remaining authentic to who you always envisioned they were. List the things that they've taught you and how they've helped you be the best version of yourself. Take a moment and reach out to these individuals if you're able to get in touch with them. Let them know what an inspiration they've been to you.

For those who have ended up being false unicorns, think of the energy that initially drew you to them. What did you feel? What did you love about them and why? Now think of whatever made you realize they were actually a rhino. Maybe it was certain values or actions that didn't feel in alignment with your own energy.

Now consider this: What could this individual have done that would have kept you feeling inspired by them? Take that information and flip the mirror onto yourself. Write down how you can take this newfound knowledge and embrace it in a way that makes *you* the unicorn. This is your takeaway and guide to how you can begin to represent a higher vibration for others.

Short-Burst Unicorns: People Who Offer Acts of Kindness at Just the Right Time

Short-burst unicorns are those who appear in moments of need, providing acts of kindness at just the right time. Maybe it was someone who was there to help you change a flat tire when you were stranded, a nurse who assisted you at a difficult time, or someone who randomly passed along a book with a message that you really needed at that moment. There are so many possibilities for amazing moments from single and fleeting connections.

For me, one example came about after a surgery. I had a volunteer come in to visit me for a short while. I was uncomfortable, foggy from drugs, and trying to wrap my head around the frustrating diagnosis of a disease that I knew didn't have a known cure. She walked in with a smile and asked if she could offer me an energy healing session. After I accepted she asked, "Is it okay if I use some essential oils? I have this blend with me today." She pulled out a green bottle and my husband started laughing. "That's her favorite!" Luke exclaimed.

A grin spread across my face. Even in all my discomfort, happiness burst through. It was indeed an oil that I adore. It always reminds me of gum I chewed as a kid and leaves me feeling in high spirits. It also always makes my mouth water, which I find funny. I could have doused myself in the whole bottle.

She proceeded to rub my feet with the oil and followed up with some energy work. By the end, I felt soothed, supported, and loved. It was exactly what I needed in that moment. I'd wanted to follow up with her and send a thank-you card, but I was never able to figure out exactly who it was that dropped in.

That's what short-burst unicorns are about. They drop a little kindness right where you most need it and go on their way. They remind us that we're worthy of the love we desire and inspire us to remind others of the same.

★ ★ ★

In this chapter, we've looked at tools of vision and reflection through which unicorn energy works its magic in an attempt to reach us: reflection, imagination, beauty, dreams, passions, personal quirks, and our unicorn people. In the next section, we'll get into even more tools that focus on the magic of color.

chapter two

Chapter Three

ADDITIONAL
UNICORN TOOLS:
COLOR &
VIBRANCE

We've looked at quite a few tools that unicorns use to get us to hear their messages so that we might experience a vibrant life. In this chapter, we'll cover some additional unicorn tools that revolve around light and beauty that's being projected at us every single day. This delight is all around in the color that surrounds us. It's an everyday magic that we take for granted because it's just the norm. The grass is green, the sky is blue ... It just is what it is, so what? But tell that to someone who is color-blind and for the first time is seeing color the way the majority of people do their entire lives.

The Power of Color

Just because color is something that's a part of our everyday lives doesn't mean it's not wonderful. It might be difficult to think of it in this way, but with a little mindfulness we can put a new perspective on something that seems ordinary. Even if you're color-blind, you can still appreciate color magic within whatever range of color you're able to see.

Imagine that you could never see red again. What is the value of that color to you? Or imagine that you could no longer see the difference between brown and green. Now picture the world in monochromatic gray or shades of brown instead of the wide range of colors you've most likely lived with throughout your life. If you've ever found yourself depressed during the dark months of gray and white winter, you might be able to easily imagine this. When we consider these kinds of limitations, the power of color becomes more apparent.

For those who actually are color-blind and are unable to see the difference between certain colors, there are glasses available that can help them see what the average person experiences every day. If you've ever known anyone in this situation or seen a video of someone seeing color magic for the first time, or if you've experienced it yourself, you'll know it's a very emotional moment of wonder, appreciation, amazement, and even disbelief. "You see this beauty all the time? This is incredible! How is this real? I don't believe it." These are some common exclamations. Sometimes no words come as the person's breath is taken away by a vibrant world. For those who already naturally see the full range of color, witnessing this puts it into a new perspective. It's not just green ... it's dazzling emerald, rich forest green, and lime turning to yellow in the sparkling sunlight.

Rainbows and Unicorns

Another way to think of the power of color is to recall a moment when you saw a rainbow. In that rare moment, you probably felt a thrill from seeing color in this specific kind of way. It may have been surprising, thrilling, breathtaking, or all of the above. But why were you more excited by this sort of color appearance than with all the other color that's around you? It's because a rainbow takes color out of the ordinary and presents it to you in a new way.

For a short moment, from the time the rainbow appears until it slowly fades away, you pause and appreciate the magic of color.

Unicorns and rainbows are often paired together, which makes sense because rainbows are the "unicorns of color." Some of the meanings we associate with both of them are very similar. They both represent what's rarely seen and the things that catch us off guard. They can't be captured but instead are to be acknowledged and appreciated in the moment. When one is on the hunt for a unicorn, it's a difficult and holy hero's journey, shrouded in the mystery of where it might lead. The same can be said of rainbows. When they're revealed after rain, they inspire us. They're beauty and happiness following difficult times, and we're left imagining what they might lead to.

I can still recall the first time I saw a rainbow. I was four years old and my parents led Amy and me out to the front yard. "Look!" they said, pointing to the tree line across the street. Above all that wooded evergreen was a beautiful arc of color. I couldn't believe it. I imagined that I might see Rainbow Brite riding her horse across the colorful sky at any second. I stared intently, not wanting to miss it. While Rainbow Brite never appeared, there was still magic there for us to observe from afar, and that's part of what leaves a lingering sense of mystery and wonder.

The Material Rainbow: Crystals and Stones

Thankfully there are versions of the rainbow that are more tangible. For example, crystals are like holding the rainbow's encapsulated energy right in the palm of your hand.

Those who are drawn to unicorns are often captivated by gemstones, minerals, crystals, and stones as well. (For simplicity, I'll be using these terms interchangeably.) We're drawn to sparkle and shine because at our core, light is what we are, however often we may forget it. Crystals remind us of this. Having them near acts as a support on many levels, from mental, emotional, and physical to spiritual and energetic.

By their very nature, crystals help us focus on the positive through the beautiful way they catch the light and share every color imaginable. There's also an air of mystery about them. They exist in the silent spaces of this world, like a unicorn hidden deep in the shadows of the forest. When we finally find the right crystals for us, they bring a thrill. When we come across certain ones that we align with, we have that "ooooooh" moment of syncing with energy that lights us up and guides us to rise higher.

Unicorn folk appreciate the beauty and unique energy that each combination and arrangement of minerals presents. While there are innumerable types of crystals, each is fascinating in its own right, and different crystals have different creative meanings and purposes. Various benefits have been associated with crystals, from support for physical wellness to enhancement of psychic abilities.

It can be assumed that symbolism has been attributed to stones for as long as humans have been attracted to them. Even if you don't believe that crystals and stones literally impart supportive energy of specific types, the act of applying intention and affirmation toward something beautiful, solid, and right within your grasp is a proven practice. We discussed this in chapter 1 when we looked at the workings of imagination. If we pick up an amethyst in hopes of finding some quiet calm, it doesn't matter whether the crystal is sharing its energy or we are creating it on our own. Personally, I believe it's always a bit of both. Either way, it's an attainable magic. We'll look at some of these benefits soon, but first let's cover some basics of how to pick and care for your stones.

Selecting Stones Like a Unicorn

There are a plethora of stones available to you. You could walk outside right now and find a natural stone at random to help you connect with the earth and your rhythm in it. If that feels right to you, go for it! I have a selection of stones that I've collected like this throughout the years that bring me grounding and inspiration.

However, when you gather stones this way, consider the space and take a moment to ask the stone if it's okay for you to remove it. This can be done by holding the stone in your hands, closing your eyes, and tuning in to how you feel. Pay attention to whether there is a positive vibration or buzz running through your body. Notice whether you feel pulled forward just a bit.

These are indications that the stone has connected positively with you. On the other hand, if you feel nothing or there's a sense that you're being pushed backward, the stone should remain where you found it.

Various benefits have been associated with crystals, from support for physical wellness to enhancement of psychic abilities.

chapter three

Sometimes the best thing we can do is simply connect with energy at the source and take that as the gift, instead of trying to physically haul it with us. Taking from rivers, beaches, and other spaces that aren't our property can negatively impact these places. In Hawaii, Pele's Curse warns us not to remove native materials from the island, lest we be haunted by bad luck. Pele is the goddess of fire and volcanoes, and it's said that she honors lava rocks as though they're her children, becoming distressed when they're removed. This may be a modern tale and not an original Hawaiian belief, but it's certainly helped to put the importance of conservation into our consciousness. If we all take a little here and a little there, it adds up and can be destructive.

If you do choose to remove natural stones, act in the way of a forager for wild plants by keeping in mind the importance of not overdoing it. Take only what you need and leave the rest to sustain the space and other foragers to come. If you do choose to take a stone, consider giving something in return. Search for litter that can be removed so that you're exchanging energy and healing the land instead of just taking from it.

Aside from gathering naturally found stones that you're drawn to, obtaining crystals and gemstones can be a personal sort of quest. In the same way that specific herbs, flowers, or essential oils call to us in relation to individual maladies, certain crystals and gemstones speak to specific energy needs. I've chosen to share the list of stones later in this chapter because they spoke up as I meditated on the characteristics and attributes of unicorn energy.

If you don't have access to any of the crystals I mention here, it's okay. Don't feel that you need to go out and buy any or all of these items. Consider those that you already have access to. Really, any stone that brings you the "good feels" could be included in this list. At the top would be the one that you are most intensely magnetized to and that makes you feel a sense of intrigue. If you have a favorite stone that you already adore, there is excellent energy available there for you to work with. Or if anyone has gifted you a crystal recently, that may be the exact one that's calling to you.

If you decide you'd love to obtain a stone that you don't already have, the list I provide in this chapter can be a good place to start. New practices can be inspired by new tools.

Just remember that unicorns tread lightly. Take care in how you source your materials. This can be a challenge with crystals and gemstones since the industry isn't regulated in a transparent way yet, unfortunately. You can ask store owners if they're aware of fair trade or mining practices for the stones they have available to help you choose your items in a more informed way.

With the purchase of new stones, be aware of the tendency to overconsume. In our society, we are constantly taught to desire more, more, and more. It can be fun and inspiring to work with new tools, but if you're in a coveting mindset instead of an inspirational one, it might be better to work with what you already have initially and then see if you still feel the desire to include new items in your practice. If you feel overwhelmed or indecisive or experience shallow breathing when you're trying to make your choice of purchase, these are all signs that the crystals you're considering may not be the right ones for you.

To some, it may seem silly to practice this level of mindfulness when choosing crystals, even communing with them as living beings. But by selecting them in this way, we're abiding by the philosophy of "do no harm." We're treading gently in the forest as a unicorn would, looking out for the other creatures that are more vulnerable than us. While this normally applies to living things, our earth is a living body and stones make up her bones. What we do to her, we do to ourselves. By acting compassionately toward even a stagnant rock, it will become more automatic for us to save the bee we find struggling in a birdbath, move the spider we find inside to the outdoors, skip the gossip, extend a helping hand to others, and practice similar acts of kindness toward ourselves.

Here are some tips for choosing stones like a unicorn:

- Connect energetically with the stone and ask if it's okay for you to remove it from its natural environment.

- Honor conservation efforts, and especially don't take from prohibited areas.

- If you take a stone, give something in return as an exchange of energy. One idea is to pick up litter that you find.

- Work with the crystals you already have.

- When acquiring new crystals, try to find ethical sources.

- Connect with your crystal to discover what its unique meaning is for you.

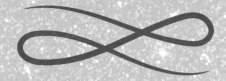

TIP 7

★ ★ ★

Choosing Stones Like a Unicorn

- Connect energetically with the stone and ask if it's okay for you to remove it from its natural environment.
- Honor conservation efforts, and especially don't take from prohibited areas.
- If you take a stone, give something in return as an exchange of energy. One idea is to pick up litter that you find.
- Work with the crystals you already have.
- When acquiring new crystals, find ethical sources.
- Connect with your crystal to discover what its unique meaning is for you.

Caring for Your Crystals and Stones

There are various ways to take care of your stones. Smoke cleansing (with sage, sweetgrass, or palo santo, for example), water cleansing, and sunbathing are a few options, but the ones that better align with unicorn energy are moon bathing and earth grounding. These are the ways I prefer to cleanse my stones. Just as unicorns are mesmerized and energized by their own reflection, crystals also recharge in the light of the moon, our mirror of the night. This cleansing method is as easy as leaving your stones on a windowsill where they will regularly receive both sunlight and moonlight.

Alternately, returning stones to the earth connects them directly with their original source of energy. Think of it like going home after being away for a long time. You can breathe a sigh of relief, rest, and gently recharge in your own environment. Dig a shallow spot in your garden, landscaping, or other preferred spot, and let your stones recharge for a moon cycle. Just don't forget to mark where you buried them. If you don't have a yard, you can dig a spot in one of your houseplants and set the stones where they can receive the moonlight.

As a sidenote, if you ever decide to let go of any of your stones and you don't want to give them away, returning them to the earth is the most respectful option.

Ten Stand-Out Crystals and Stones

Let's take a look now at a collection of ten stand-out crystals that have a range of physical and spiritual properties. These stones have mesmerizing beauty, purification abilities, high vibration, the ability to amplify energy, and more.

I'll be sharing some of the various meanings and associations for each stone, including their associated chakras. Some of this information comes from the insight of others and some of it comes from my own experience and understanding. It's especially useful to determine what each crystal means for you specifically. Don't take my or other people's word for it; feel it for yourself. You can do this in the same way that I shared earlier in this chapter for connecting with a stone in its natural environment to see if it's the right one for you.

This list includes ametrine, azurmalachite, clear quartz, fluorite, labradorite, moonstone, opal, peacock ore, pyrite, and shungite. This is not an all-inclusive list. There may be other crystals you're drawn to that aren't included here, so think of this as a jumping-off point for intriguing options.

AMETRINE: Ametrine is a stone of empowered metamorphosis and authentic knowing. It blends purple bands of amethyst and golden yellow/brown bands of citrine, which are both quartz stones.

Amethyst is a stone of security, transformation, and vision. It's often a "first grab" stone when a person is going through a difficult situation. It helps bring a sense of soothing calm in the same way that lavender flower or essential oil does. While things may be tumultuous or uncertain, amethyst reminds us to pause, take a breath, and find the inner strength to change negative habits. This stone provides a sense of steadiness and security in the root chakra. This groundedness allows us to think beyond basic security, clearing the way to focus on lighter vibrations. As a stone aligned with the third eye, amethyst is also useful for dreamwork and connecting with your natural intuition.

Citrine is a stone of self-confidence, happiness, and courage. Like amethyst, it supports willpower and change, but instead of calming, it brings a burst of cheery sunshine energy. If a smile were a stone, citrine would be it. You might think of its color as a match to a lion's mane. Like a lion, citrine reminds us to come back to our core power at the sacral chakra and take hold of our courage. It helps to illuminate what's been holding us back so we can move past self-sabotage to choose lighter and more abundant things.

The combination of these two complementary-colored stones has a dramatic and balancing effect. Together, they align us with both our authentic self at the solar plexus and our sense of vision at the third eye, helping us to tap into our divine guidance and manifest what we envision for ourselves.

If you don't have ametrine, you can make use of individual amethyst and citrine. If you have only one available, call on the energy of whichever stone you're missing from the combination.

Chakras: Root, but especially the solar plexus and third eye.

AZURMALACHITE: Azurmalachite is a stone of objective awareness and a balanced combination of power and calm. I first encountered azurmalachite when I was at an exhibit at the Denver Museum of Nature and Science in Colorado. It stopped me in my tracks. Hypnotized, I was soon left behind as the group I was with moved along without me. While I'd seen both azurite and malachite before, the combination of the two together had an enhanced and mesmerizing effect. The rich inky blue set against a vivid green is reminiscent of the deep ocean along a tropical landscape or the earth from a great distance. Azurmalachite provides perspective and helps us move past blocks set by the ego, allowing us to be more flexible and receptive.

Azurite has historically been used for its blue pigment. Like watching the ocean, it has a calming effect that supports an opening to communication and intuition.

Malachite has also been used for its (green) pigment. It is more grounding in its visual association to earth rather than water.

Azurmalachite represents our connection to both the earth and what lies beyond, and is a reminder that we can connect to both worlds. It supports us in remaining grounded while also rising to attain higher spiritual wisdom.

If you don't have azurmalachite, you can make use of individual azurite and malachite. If you have only one available, call on the energy of whichever stone you are missing from the combination.

Chakras: Heart, throat, third eye, and crown.

CLEAR QUARTZ: Clear quartz is a stone of energy, focus, and amplification. We know this in a very tangible way because many of our electronic devices use quartz crystals for something called piezoelectric energy. This is a charge that builds up in certain materials like bone, DNA, silk, some ceramics, and crystals when they're put under mechanical stress. By converting mechanical energy into a usable form of electricity with the help of crystals, we're making use of crystal magic in our everyday lives. Think about your daily uses of quartz. Perhaps it's by keeping time with your quartz watch, sharing a musical greeting card, or using a cell phone.

In the introduction to her book *Crystals Beyond Beginners*, Margaret Ann Lembo explains the possibilities of this crystal beautifully, saying, "Quartz crystals were used in the earliest radio receivers and were at the heart of telecommunication equipment in the 1940s. Today, we know that we can tune into certain radio channels or stabilize a particular frequency to receive a broadcast. When we apply that same basic principle to our connection with the spiritual realm, we can use a quartz crystal to help us stay focused during meditation by stabilizing our frequency or tuning into cosmic forces by 'turning the dial'" (Lembo 2019).

A laser wand is crystal quartz that forms in a longer shape; it's wider at the base and narrows to a pointed end. It is an enhanced version of the quartz crystal, providing an even finer level of focus and attraction. It conducts, attunes,

and attracts. Clear quartz with a point at the end can also have this kind of focused effect. Think of it as your own personal unicorn horn! Hold it to your forehead and you may be able to visualize its vibrations moving through your body or even hear its tuning fork–like hum.

Some other quartz crystals that I'm especially drawn to include iris/rainbow quartz, a crystal that shimmers and flashes rainbow colors due to internal refraction of light, and spirit quartz, a stone that's encrusted with a layer of smaller crystals on its surface in dazzling fashion.

Whether you have a laser wand or an alternate form of this crystal, use quartz to cleanse your energy body, bring clarity for dreams, or tune into your spirit guides during meditation. Just like a prism breaks up a rainbow of light, clear quartz carries within it the potential for all color. It's a crystal that could serve as an excellent basis for your collection.

Chakras: All chakras, but especially the crown. A quartz laser wand would apply even more to the third eye.

FLUORITE: Fluorite is a stone of illumination, mental focus, and play. It appears in a wide range of colors, from golden-yellow or green to pink, purple, and blue. You're likely to find it in rainbow bands, especially of green/blue, dark to lilac purple, and clear layers that look like they've been captured in ice (which is mainly the version I'm referencing here). The colors move with ease from one to the next. The transitional layers speak to fluorite's association with transformation and going with the flow, allowing hardened emotions to move freely once again. Instead of getting caught up in strongly held ideals, you can use fluorite to help you open up to realize the bigger picture of things, which can aid in positive communication and spiritual connection.

Looking at the polished and colorful form of fluorite brings to mind sweet suckers and sugary rock candy. On the one hand, it has a whimsical playfulness about it, but on the other, there's a sure-footed, steady strength that is unmoving and focused. Its transparent nature is symbolic of having mental clarity and heightened intuitive vision in order to see through falsehoods.

An amazing aspect of some forms of fluorite is that it can give off light in certain circumstances, such as when it's under ultraviolet light, subjected to heat (thermoluminescence), or crushed or pulled apart (triboluminescence). This luminescent quality is a reminder that you have incredible strength and inner wisdom that you can rely on during times of great challenge. Even in the most trying times, your light shines through.

If you don't have fluorite, you can make use of ametrine for its similar color transitions and attention to the third eye, as well as peacock ore for its vibrant sense of play.

Chakras: Heart, throat, and crown, but mostly the third eye.

LABRADORITE: Labradorite is a stone of new perspectives, euphoric inspiration, and heightened possibility. It has a metallic rainbow iridescence (most often appearing in green, blue, and gold) that's reminiscent of the aurora borealis.

Imagine you're outside in the dark of night and suddenly the northern lights appear unexpectedly. You stop what you're doing and stare intently at the sky with complete focus. The hair stands up on your arms. Your mouth gapes open in awe just before a smile stretches across your face. Maybe you laugh or exclaim your surprise and joy out loud. You're caught and captivated by a magical sort of beauty. There's no room for logic or overthinking. You're in the moment and feeling straight from the heart. It's breathtaking, stunning, and mysterious.

That feeling is everything that labradorite is about. There's euphoria in it. It helps you raise your vibration, allowing you to better access your psychic abilities. It also helps in bridging the gap between our lower vibrations and spirit's higher vibration in order to achieve better communication. It encourages you to look beyond your usual narrow perspective and see a more expansive vision. Labradorite doesn't just shine across the shadows; it catches those shadows off guard so that you might see them in an entirely different light.

If you don't have labradorite, you could instead use moonstone or opal, as they have the same mystical iridescence and nighttime associations.

Chakras: Heart, third eye, and crown.

MOONSTONE: Moonstone is a stone of creativity, transition, intuition, and reflection. It helps us awaken to what was previously hidden or avoided. It is a cloudy silver-white, with an iridescent rainbow effect, as though glitter is shimmering within it. Moonstone is a gentle stone that guides us to reconnect with the nurturing energy that's available to us through celestial cycles, nature's rhythm, and the divine feminine.

What unhealthy patterns have you fallen into? Moonstone can help you find flexibility and bring to light things that need changing. When you're able to find a pace that better aligns with your natural rhythm, your sense of creativity can flourish with as much ease as the moon turning full or the spring raising flowers.

Moonstone is also a great ally in the development of psychic abilities, especially psychic vision through dreamwork and the awakening of the third eye. Try placing a moonstone on your third

chapter three

eye before you meditate. Pay attention to what you feel, and see if you're presented with any insightful visions. Or set it on your nightstand or under your pillow before you go to bed. When you wake up, write down any prominent imagery or wisdom that you can remember. By applying conscious focus to these areas, you're strengthening your energetic muscles. This allows your psychic abilities to grow and eventually become more second-nature.

If you don't have moonstone, you could instead use labradorite or opal, as they both have a similar iridescence.

Chakras: Solar plexus and crown, but most prominently the sacral and third eye.

OPAL: Opal is a stone of wonder, attraction, and hopeful comfort. It comes in various forms, but the ones I'm most drawn to are those with a milky-white base and speckles of rainbow color alighting from within. This rainbow iridescence plays like the reflection of light on water or the shining flecks of a sunset hitting the clouds just so. It's amazing the way it's soft and subtle while also being flashy and captivating.

Opal has an attraction that draws energy in like a moth to a flame. When I was a kid, I remember sneaking into my grandma's bedroom every time I went to visit so I could admire her opal pendant dangling on a necklace hanger. At some point I'd been warned of its delicate nature, so I knew not to touch it, but I would stand close by and admire it longingly. It had a hypnotic beauty that I simply wanted to be near.

I imagine the personality of opal to be like that of a dolphin. It's playful and a little mischievous, sparking the imagination and a childlike sense of creativity. Like dolphins surprising boat-goers with a swim-along party, this stone fills us with a sense of awe and sucks us right into *this very moment*, setting us firmly in the present.

Part of opal's hypnotic nature has to do with its sense of movement. Its colors glide, morph, and blend, seeming to rise and shift on a tide, which makes sense since opals contain water. Just as water moves in waves, opal supports us through the ups and downs of emotional shifts and life transitions.

TIP 8

★ ★ ★

Learn the Meaning of Your Crystal

To determine what a stone means for you, hold it in your hands and feel its energy. If you feel a welcoming buzz, ask it about its purpose. Listen for any key words that pop into your head, feel for emotions that bubble up, and watch for imagery that appears in your mind's eye. These are all clues to how you and your crystal can work together.

Opal is a delicate stone and shouldn't be left in hot areas where it might crack or dry out. There are imitations available, like opalite, which you don't need to be as careful with since it's made from a glassy substance. Opalites are still intriguing, with a milky, opalescent quality that feels very reminiscent of pop culture's lavender-pink and soft-blue representation of all things unicorn, but if you're looking for natural opal, be aware that there is a difference.

If you don't have opal, you could instead use labradorite or moonstone for their similar iridescent quality and play of light and color.

Chakras: Solar plexus and third eye, but most prominently the sacral, heart, and crown.

PEACOCK ORE: Peacock ore is a stone of playfulness, expression, and confidence. It reminds us to revel in our creativity while also remaining grounded. It supports authentic expression without apology. If you need more color in your life, this is the stone for you. With a mix of mainly blue, teal, purple, and raspberry, this stone is a wild burst of fun.

Peacock ore can be found naturally in the form of bornite, but in order to enhance the effect of its iridescent tarnish, treated versions of bornite or chalcopyrite are frequently available under the same name. With all the other nine stones listed here, I've intentionally focused on the items that are found in their natural form. But in this case, I make an exception, because peacock ore is symbolic of times when we need to put in extra effort to achieve our full potential. For example, many of us end up having a difficult time reconnecting with our true self in order to find the things that make us happy to our core. We can get by, but if we dig for the source of that richer joy, life can be more of a thrill.

Peacock ore reminds us of the playful nature we all have within that's just waiting to be tapped for enhanced effect. In that playfulness is the map to our simple pleasures. Whatever it may be, the activity is its own achievement, as in fun for fun's sake. There isn't any real goal attached to it, or if there is, it's a side benefit.

If you don't have peacock ore, you could instead use pyrite, as they're both grounding, attuned to energy of the solar plexus, and iron-rich, with an appealing shine.

Chakras: Root and third eye, but especially the sacral, solar plexus, and throat.

PYRITE: Pyrite is a stone of creativity, self-worth, and knowing your true self. If you've ever held pyrite, you know that it has weight to it and thus is very grounding. Also known as "fool's gold," pyrite reminds us to find the magic in what is considered ordinary. While pyrite is not the same as true gold, it's still very beautiful. In fact, I find pyrite to be much more beautiful than gold. Its metallic copper color sparkles in the light and asks us to find the creative shine in our lives.

Pyrite is a stone of the solar plexus, where we address falsehoods in order to know who we truly are. This stone wants us to recognize our true value and reminds us that we're worthy of love and all the good things we desire. Historically, pyrite was used to start a fire by striking two pieces of it together to create a spark. What is the spark in you that needs igniting? Pyrite helps you know who you are at your core so you can fan that spark into a full flame of golden truth and authentic aspiration.

If you don't have pyrite, you could instead use peacock ore, as they're both iron-rich, with an appealing metallic shine.

Chakras: Root and sacral, but especially the solar plexus.

SHUNGITE: Shungite is a stone of purification, regeneration, and protection. It's currently only known to exist in Russia and is sometimes called "the stone of life." It's not a crystal but instead is a rock that contains lots of carbon and silicon dioxide, along with other minerals. It looks a lot like coal, but unlike coal, shungite has been found to contain something called fullerenes. These are very stable closed cages of atoms that resemble a soccer ball. Before this realization, fullerenes were known only in human-made form. Just think about that. Something that we thought existed only in our own imagination had been waiting hidden in nature for us to find. There's something very unicorn-like about that! Fullerenes have potential applications in science, technology, and medicine, and we're still learning about all their possible benefits.

Shungite has antioxidant and anti-inflammatory effects (Sajo et al. 2017). It has a high level of absorption for contaminants like heavy metals, ammonia, and pesticides, and is thirty times more effective than activated carbon in removing free radicals from water. In addition, it is antibacterial. To apply these benefits, consumers have used shungite in topical skincare products and in water treatment or infusion. (These applications are still being researched, so any kind of topical or ingestive use is not recommended here without guidance from your healthcare provider.) All of this makes shungite excellent for water treatment and purification. It can also be a good conductor and has the ability to help block radiation that comes from electromagnetics (EMFs) and radio sources (Mosin and Ignatov 2013). Pretty impressive!

While shungite's properties might seem too good to be true (or even as fantastical as a unicorn purifying and healing with the touch of its magical horn), this stone has a no-nonsense air about it. It doesn't try to impress in any way. Its dull, dark color is grounding and calls to mind a person rolling up their sleeves, ready to get down to business and take care of whatever needs to be done.

Chakras: Root and sacral.

• EXERCISE 9 •
Find Your Unicorn Crystal

Let's take a moment for you to discover your unicorn crystal. Did one of the stones I mentioned in the previous list seem to jump out at you in some way? It's also possible that your personal unicorn crystal might be something else entirely that you have yet to discover. There are so many more possibilities!

To consider which crystal or stone you feel most aligned with, gather visuals of the possibilities. Look at crystal and stone books, search online, go to rock shops, or search out in nature. Watch out for that "zing" that tells you you've found something special. It could be your attraction to something about the crystal's appearance, the symbol or meaning associated with it, or the energy connection that draws you to it.

If you still aren't sure, try this. Sit quietly for a moment, breathing in and out slowly, with your eyes closed. Rest your hands on your knees, with your palms facing up. Once you feel relaxed, imagine that you can feel the weight of the stone. To keep energy balanced on both sides of your body, imagine that you have two stones, one resting in each hand. Sense the energy that your stone is sharing with you. After a bit, visualize what it looks like. Notice whether it's raw or polished. Pay attention to its color, density, and opacity. Once you've familiarized yourself with the appearance of your stone, ask it why it has come to you. What is its symbolic and energetic purpose? How does that serve your needs at this time? If your stone's purpose isn't clearly revealed, it's okay. It will reveal itself over time.

As you return from your meditation, write down the things you felt and noticed. Is it clear which stone was calling to you? Is it one that you already have or one that you've come across in your research? If not, try to find it, or just keep it in mind

As you meditate on what crystal is best for you in this moment, don't be surprised if your unicorn guide shows up.

in case one day you do come across it. If you can't find or identify the exact stone, it could be that yours is one that hasn't been discovered yet. For example, true rainbow quartz (versus titanium quartz, which is an artificially coated version) was only recently discovered in 2009. There may yet be others waiting to be unearthed. And if that's the case, you can continue to connect with it through meditation or you can search for other stones that have similar characteristics to take its place for now.

As you meditate on what crystal is best for you in this moment, don't be surprised if your unicorn guide shows up. The first of my unicorns presented itself with wings decorated with gemstones that changed according to what message she had for me. (She obviously knew I'm a sucker for symbolism.) Even if your unicorn doesn't appear bejeweled in stones, they may appear during your visualization to help you discover what your very own unicorn stone is all about.

For me, labradorite takes the cake. To my eyes, this is simply the most beautiful stone that exists. When I'm near it, I'm hypnotized. The first time I encountered labradorite was just after my college graduation, when it was given to me as a gift in pendant form. At the time, I was ending one academic journey, but I would soon embark on a new one centered on everything that labradorite is about. Its purpose was to guide me in following my alternative interests in spirituality, psychic ability, and healing. This pendant continues to connect with me as a reminder to watch for the things that bring me a sense of wonder.

I've learned about many other stones since then, and I always wonder if I might stumble across something that will steal my favor, but nothing ever has. There's just something about labradorite that remains steady for me. Still, it's entirely possible that a new favorite will one day take its place, and I remain open to new possibilities.

• EXERCISE 10 •

Make Your Own Unicorn Energy Mist

When the idea for this book first hit me, inclusion of a unicorn energy mist was a very prominent item that came to mind. There was no ignoring this idea. I immediately knew the ingredients list and other details around it. "Sure, okay," I thought. "That sounds like it could be fun." But I didn't fully understand its context. What made this a "unicorn" practice anyway? I wasn't sure there was enough to it.

As it turns out, while making a unicorn mist was the very first practice that struck me, it was one of the last ones that I ended up writing about. As the rest of the book unfolded, I began to understand more of the reasoning behind why this practice was to be included, and I was excited to try it out for myself. Unicorn characteristics and tools come into play here. The beauty of nature is included in the mist, with essential oils, flower essences, and crystals and stones. And imagination plays a part through visualization, tying it all together.

Working with ingredients and recipes is a playful, creative, and engaging act. It's a process where you build up energy and anticipation. This begins with setting an intention for the recipe's purpose and the outcome you hope to achieve by using it. With your imagination, you envision the end result. And when the final product has been put together, you have a physical representation of something that previously existed only in your mind. These are all things that make up sacred rituals and magic spells, as well as your grandma's famous cookies! And like those delicious cookies, you're left with something that lingers and can provide continued enjoyment.

Another reason why this mist is useful has to do with synchronicity of energy. We're creating a concoction that has a higher vibration than that of your physical body and, as a result, can encourage your energy to rise. This is because the presence of one frequency has an effect on another. This can be seen with clocks and with body rhythms such as heart and breathing rates. Two clocks swinging a pendulum at different rates of oscillation will eventually fall into the same rhythm. Heartbeats and breathing rates of loved ones often fall in sync with one another as well. There's a vibrational signal that aligns energy into synchronized movement. Vibration and frequency feel mysterious and magical because they're often beyond our understanding, but their effects are playing out all around us every single day.

Think of this unicorn energy mist as premade magic that you can use over and over again to remind you of the intention you set while making it. In this way, every time you use it, it can be a steady and slow drip of love and a tool to support your sustained high vibes and good-feels.

Unicorn Mist Ingredients

- Shungite: a small piece
- Clear crystal quartz: a small piece, preferably with a point
- A small glass spray bottle: approximately 3–4 ounces in size
- Clean water: 3–4 ounces

- Essential oils: 3–8 drops of any essential oil with purifying properties. Here are some examples:
  * Citronella
  * Frankincense
  * Lavender
  * Lemon, lime, or other citrus
  * Palo santo
  * Rose
  * Rosemary
  * Sage
  * Tea tree
- Flower essences: 1 drop of each flower essence, or visualize this using the Rose Essence Technique (which will be described shortly)
- Paper
- Tape
- A pen or marker

STONES: When I made my unicorn mist, I used a small shungite bead so it could easily fit in my glass bottle. As we learned earlier, shungite is a stone of purification, regeneration, and protection. The shungite and essential oils in this mix provide you with the purifying power of the unicorn's horn, while your pointed crystal quartz plays the part of the energy-amplifying alicorn.

ESSENTIAL OILS: Essential oil is the concentrated liquid pulled from a plant. The essential oils I've included here all have purifying properties, from antibacterial, antifungal, and antimicrobial to antiseptic and deodorizing, among other things. Citronella and tea tree are especially cleansing. Lavender provides a calming air, while citrus oils such as lemon, lime, and orange are uplifting and energizing. Historically, holy and sacred oils such as frankincense, palo santo, rosemary, and sage can add a high vibration and a spiritual intention to the mix.

Rose oil also has antibacterial properties, but I've included this one in the list not for its purification qualities but mainly because it's usually recorded as the highest-frequency oil at 320 MHz (Higley and Higley 2012, 114). To put this into perspective, lavender is 118 MHz (Ibid., 88) and a healthy human body is 62–78 MHz, and when the frequency level of the body goes down, disease begins to take hold. With rose being at such a high level, it's an optimal oil to choose for a unicorn mist. The downside is that it's also very expensive. No worries, though. If you'd like to include the high vibration of this flower but can't obtain the essential oil, we'll be looking at alternate options as we dig into putting your recipe together.

You don't need to have all of these oils to make your mist. Mix, match, and make use of those you're most drawn to from this list or use other favorites that you already have. Just make sure that the oils you're using are of good quality. This means that the plants weren't raised using things like harmful herbicides and pesticides, and

Think of this unicorn energy mist as premade magic that you can use to remind you of the intention you set while making it.

the resulting oil hasn't been cut or blended with other ingredients.

Good quality also means that the oil has been responsibly sourced. For example, palo santo is an endangered tree, and sustainable use means the oil has been produced in a way that doesn't contribute to worsening endangerment. In the case of palo santo, this might mean the oil comes only from wood that died naturally and where the supplier also plants to ensure the continuation of the tree.

Finding this kind of information can sometimes be a challenge, so you'll need to do a bit of research to find sources you trust.

Also, make sure you understand how to personally use essential oils safely. For example, citrus oils can cause extra sensitivity to the sun, and if oils aren't diluted, they can cause skin irritation. If you already know you're sensitive to any of the ingredients, don't use those items. For more on essential oil safety, please see the recommended resources at the end of the book.

FLOWER ESSENCES: Unlike essential oils, where you're using the physical matter of the plant, a flower essence is the imprinting of a flower's vibrational wisdom onto water. While essential oils make use of part of the actual plant, with flower essences you aren't left with any of the actual flower matter in your final solution, just the energy.

Using flower essences helps to harmonize our energy on the emotional and mental levels and brings things back into balance. There are a lot of different essences to match different intentions, so you can research those you are most drawn to if you decide you want to include a premade product in your unicorn mist. Or if you already have flower essences sitting in your cupboard, you can certainly grab those. I personally had a few already on hand. These included Agrimony for working through emotional pain, Aspen for trust and moving through fear, Pine for self-acceptance and letting go of past events, and Star of Bethlehem for wholeness and release of trauma. There is a plethora of flower essence formulas available.

Alternately, you could make your own flower essence with any flower you're most drawn to. Alcohol is usually used to preserve flower essence, which has never resonated with me. Logically, I understand its use for preservation, but energetically it has a harshness to it. Because of this, we'll be focusing on a different way to draw on flower essence. This is where our inclusion of rose energy will come into play. We'll look at this in more detail as we're putting our ingredients together.

Making Your Mist

First, gather your ingredients. Then find a quiet space where you can create your mist with intention. Wherever you are, try to have it be an uplifting space where you can fully relax. Put on some calming music and, if possible, sit in a sunny spot. You might even wait to do this on an extra-special day, like a favorite holiday or your birthday. Making these kinds of choices adds to the infusion of positive vibes.

First, place the shungite and clear quartz in your glass bottle. If you don't have a glass spray bottle, you could also just mix this together in a glass bowl and anoint yourself with it occasionally or keep it in spaces where you spend time, like next to your bed, by your work computer, or in your living room. Make sure you're using glass, because other materials like plastic can leach harmful substances, especially when they come into contact with essential oil.

Pour the water in your container, but leave a bit of room at the top. Add 3–8 drops of your chosen essential oil(s), depending on how strong you prefer it to be. If you're using multiple oils, you can use one drop of each. I used one drop each of frankincense, lavender, lemon, palo santo, rosemary, sage, and tea tree. This created a subtle scent, so if you want something stronger, double the amount of oils. If you have a flower essence you'd like to include, add one drop of each. I decided to forgo using the essences I had because they contained alcohol. Instead, I used the Rose Essence Technique. Even if you use a flower essence, I would encourage you to also add in this energy practice.

Rose Essence Technique

Physical tools can be very grounding and helpful for us, but visualization and energy practices can have equally powerful effects. This technique puts you in contact with the high vibration of the rose flower. It's done at the close of creating your blend to unite all of the distinct energies you've brought together in synergy, as well as to connect you to your unique mist. The practice is based on a very powerful dream I had years ago. It wasn't just any dream, but was one we could classify as a unicorn dream of great energetic impact. It's an example of the universal energy that all of us have access to. It's just waiting for us to tap into and connect with it.

Get into a comfortable position and take hold of the unicorn energy mist that you've put together. Hold it to your heart and take slow, deep breaths. When you're feeling calm, imagine that you're standing in the middle of a flower garden. The weather is still and gentle sunlight cascades around you. Take in the surrounding space. Notice that you're standing on a path that leads to a rose at one end of the garden. There's magnetism there, and the rose seems to be calling you to it. Your unicorn joins you on the path, and you rest your hand on its back. A feeling of warmth and calmness washes over you, and you take a deep breath in, then out. As you both begin to walk down the path, notice how the rose shines with a rainbow-colored iridescent light around it.

You're standing in front of the rose now, and your unicorn

remains at your side as a silent witness. Feel how the rose is asking you to trust your instincts. You oblige by gently cupping your hands around its slightly opened petals. The rose shimmers as your energy connects. It urges you on once more, and again you oblige, energetically asking it to open for you. You allow yourself to become a vessel, and you see the white light of universal energy filling you up from your crown. The energy moves down through your body and through your hands to the rose. In response, the rose gladly unfurls its petals, as if it's breathing in the energy you've offered to it. Glittering energy moves from it to you, and back again. You ask the rose to close now and watch as its petals pull back in.

Continue this dance of opening and closing with a continued exchange of energy and glimmering light for as long as you wish. When you feel ready to move on, envision a dew drop slowly emerging from the fragrant center of the rose, like a teardrop. It trickles toward the outer edge of the petals. Just as it's ready to fall, you hold your bottle up to collect the rose's offering. Notice how your mist shimmers as the rose flower essence makes contact with it, just as the rose has shimmered throughout your energy exchange. You bow in thanks and take a step back. Your unicorn touches its spiraled horn to the rose. The flower's light dims and it closes its petals, as if going into a quiet sleep. When all feels complete, bid your unicorn farewell and gently bring yourself back to the present, with your mist still at your heart.

In my experience of this dream, I was in total awe. There was nothing else that existed but me and the rose. The feeling was indescribable, overwhelming, and it stuck with me long after I woke. The distilled expressions of the experience were a heightened sense of love, euphoria for a grand connection, and honor for receiving such a willing exchange of energy and reciprocated respect. When I put this into practice during a meditation to make my own mist, the rose shimmered at the end like a diamond, sprinkling glitter around me. At the same time, in my physical space the sun broke out of the clouds and shone brighter than it had all day. When I sprayed the mist into the air for the first time, the droplets caught the sun and made a mini-rainbow, adding to the sense of magic. "The unicorns must approve!" I thought.

Make a mental note of whether these were the same things you felt or if there was anything more you would add. You can make use of that information in the next step of setting an intention.

Applying an Intention to Your Mist

The final piece is applying your intention to your unicorn mist. This clarifies the purpose or intended outcome that you wish for when you use your mist. It could be an affirmation or mantra that you recite every time you use your mist, such as "I am open to receiving the magic that's available to me" or "My energy is vibrant, pure, and strong." Maybe your intention has to do with gratitude, humility, joy, or renewal, or it could be something else entirely. Whatever you decide you'd like to say, write it on a piece of paper along with the words "Unicorn Energy Mist" and tape it to your bottle. You could also write down the ingredients you used so you have a record of what it contains. That way you'll be able to recreate your mist if it's a version you end up especially loving.

How to Use Your Mist

Congratulations! You've successfully created your very own unicorn energy mist. To use, shake the bottle to make sure all the ingredients are well mixed, then spray it on in the morning to set your intention before you head into your activities or apply it at night to clear yourself from the events of the day. If there's something especially frustrating that you're dealing with or a "heavy" feeling in your physical environment, spray your mist around to cleanse the event or space. Use your mist before meditating and whenever you're trying to raise unicorn energy, especially when you practice the activities in this book. Think of it as wiping out the energetic cobwebs of your environment, boosting the energy around you, and leaving a little sparkle in its wake.

★ ★ ★

In this chapter and the last, we've gotten a glimpse of quite a few tools that unicorn energy works its magic through in an attempt to reach you. Hopefully some of the practices from these chapters will help you find the tools that inspire you most. From guidance through synchronicities and dreamwork to passions, crystals, your unicorn people, and more, there are so many possibilities for where you might find inspiration.

If you aren't paying attention though, you might miss those opportunities for connecting with magic when it arises. In the next chapter, we'll cover things that help us to be awake to the magic of unicorns, ensuring we're present and open to receiving all the goodness that's coming our way.

Chapter Four

BEING AWAKE TO THE MAGIC

If magic is happening all around and you aren't taking notice, it may as well not even be present. Being mindful is a key piece of connecting to unicorn energy. Mindfulness practices can help you better recognize those moments, whether they're the little things or the big things in life. In this chapter, we'll also take a look at what it means to authentically *believe* in a way that allows you to recognize the unicorn, instead of seeing a horse in its place. And finally, we'll look at how your environment is an important piece of what either helps or hinders you from seeing clearly the magic that's available to you.

Are You Noticing?

There are many reasons why we might not notice or acknowledge our unicorns when they cross our path. The most obvious reason is distraction. We're so caught up in the details of our busy lives that our unicorns are simply passed by and remain in the background. The irony is that unicorns are more likely to appear when our minds are otherwise occupied. This is sometimes their best chance to slip past the gates of judgment that normally guard against them. The grand idea you've been grasping at finally hits you out of the blue as you're singing in the shower. The answer to a problem you've been struggling with bubbles to the surface while you're taking a jog. When you're caught by surprise by a unicorn, you're able to catch sight of new realizations and insights that you might not otherwise have been receptive to. So how do we pay attention even when we aren't paying attention?

Mindfulness, Awareness, and Focused Attention

The trick here is to work on training ourselves so that we more automatically focus our attention to catch meaningful moments whenever they arise. We can do this by practicing mindful attention through meditation. With time, mindfulness programming will be running in the background of your life, helping you to notice and be more awake to magic in whatever form, and at whatever moment, it manifests for you.

Mindfulness is the practice of bringing your attention to the present moment. Being in the moment means you're just in it. You're not judging it. If you're writing, you're not filtering or worrying about how things will come together in the end; you're just letting whatever comes come. If you decide to practice mindful breathing, you're focusing on the inhale, the exhale, the inhale, the exhale, and nothing more. If you're doing the dishes, you're feeling the warmth of the water, the solidness of the plate in your hand, and the sensation of rubbing a washcloth across the smooth surface.

In all of these examples, stray thoughts and external distractions will come in and out of your awareness. With mindfulness practice, you allow those stray occurrences to be released instead of latching onto them and running a hamster wheel around them. You see it, acknowledge it, and let it go. This can be a lot harder than it sounds. Time and practice eventually make it easier. And as with any other skill, with practice you'll be more prepared to make use of this strengthened ability, even at unexpected times.

This doesn't mean you need to try to be thinking constantly about potential "sightings" that are about to come. In fact, that would leave you trapped in anticipation and obsessing about the future. The goal instead is to achieve a state of mindful presence where you're "in the now" in a way that allows you to catch unicorn moments, even when you haven't been anticipating them.

In our previous example of taking a jog, as a mindfulness practice you might pay attention to the feel of your feet in your shoes and how they hit the pavement. You notice the cool morning air on your skin, the bird that swoops by, and the pace of your breathing. And when seemingly random thoughts pass through your mind, you notice those too, but you go back to focusing on your breath. This all might seem like an uneventful time out running, but if you notice that bird is a red cardinal, a bird that you rarely see and that you associate with your deceased mother, it becomes a unicorn moment. Maybe you second-guess whether this is a sign from her, but then you notice over the next few days that cardinals keep popping up in your life in other unexpected ways: in a card from a coworker, on the cover of a book a friend passes along to you, and on a flyer a store clerks gives you as you're leaving the store. Because you're mindful, you notice these instances and acknowledge them. Eventually you accept the message as a sign of reassurance and love.

In my own example, throughout the writing of this book I was always listening to music. A dozen or more times as I was writing a word or phrase, the lyrics of a song would match it exactly. It was uncanny. The first couple of times it happened, I had that unicorn-moment feeling of shock, although it was mixed with skepticism. Even though doubt was present, I still acknowledged the moment. Especially early on in the process, I was worried that I wasn't a good enough writer. The synchronicities felt like a message of encouragement. Eventually, when it happened at so many key moments, I accepted it as a sign of support. Most recently, as I was writing the example of the cardinals appearing as a sign of reassurance, lyrics sang out declaring that birds come by to say that we're not alone. Who is it that's trying to cast aside my worries and let me know I'm on the right path? We can just say it's the unicorns.

• EXERCISE 11 •

Alicorn Meditation for Single-Pointed Focus

This is an exercise you can do for your mindfulness practice. Think of this as your unicorn-horn meditation for a concentrated and focused energy. You'll be homing in on a single point. Get it?

First, you'll want to pick something that you can focus on. What will your alicorn be? Two good options are your breath or a lit candle. Next, set a timer so you won't be distracted by wondering how long you've been meditating or if you're almost done. You can start with two minutes as a goal and try to work your way up to twenty minutes over the span of a month or two. Or you could jump right in with a longer time and see how you do. Just know that you probably will be not-so-great at this when you first start out, so don't lose hope or give up. After all, you wouldn't be able to play the violin or hit home runs without practice first. We are human and we have distractible and wandering minds that want to think, think, overthink, and think some more. Give it time; you will see improvement.

For both versions of this meditation, find a quiet and comfortable space. If you've decided to go with a candle, go ahead and light it safely. Settle in and focus on the flame. As you do, allow your breath to slow and your body to relax. Pay attention to the details of the flame: how the inner ring of color differs from the outer one, the way the flame dances and moves when it catches your breath, and even the warmth that you feel from it. While you're staring at the flame, you aren't contemplating how long it's been burning or when it might go out; you're simply observing the light.

If you've decided to go with a focus on your breath, then place a hand on your stomach. Take a breath in and feel it expand all the way down so that your hand rises with the movement. We tend to take shallow breaths, so we're starting out by intentionally taking deeper breaths. Hold the breath for a count

The goal is to achieve a state of mindful presence where you're "in the now" in a way that allows you to catch unicorn moments.

of four, then exhale on the same count. Feel the movement of your hand as you inhale and exhale.

After you've done this for a while and are starting to feel more relaxed, switch your breathing a bit. Instead of inhaling and exhaling on the same count of four, switch your focus to just the exhale. After your next inhale, put your attention on fully exhaling all of the carbon dioxide in your lungs. Feel the way your navel seems to pull all the way back to your spine when you do this. Once you feel your lungs are completely empty, allow your body to take in fresh oxygen for however long feels most natural. Don't force a certain count. Just feel into the pace your body sets for the inhale. You'll probably notice that you breathe more easily and your breath moves all the way to the expansion of your stomach. Keep up this cycle with your focus on fully exhaling.

A note of caution: Breathwork can lead to dizziness, so make sure you're not overdoing it and you're in a safe space. If you start to feel lightheaded, ease off and allow yourself to come back to balance before continuing.

As you do either of these versions, when random thoughts sneak in about what went on during your day, what you still have to do, what you're going to eat for dinner, or how you don't have time for this, or you hear the neighbor's dog, a honking horn, etc., just come back to the light or your breath. It doesn't matter if it happens one time or fifty. Even if you find that you've wandered for most of the session, come back for whatever amount of time is left. And remember, your practice now will help to improve your practice the next time.

• EXERCISE 12 •
Actively Catching the Unicorn

Mindful encouragement and mindful acknowledgment are two keys to help you catch sight of unicorns.

Mindful Encouragement

There are different things you can do to encourage your mindful attention, which translates to noticing your unicorn moments when they appear. You could put notes reminding you to focus where you'll see them, especially in places where you tend to get overly distracted. For example, the first thing I see when I walk into my work space is a letter board that says "Just breathe" on it. It reminds me of the breathwork practice and not to forget myself in the spinning of oh-so-many plates as I go about my day. You could also set a scheduled time to practice your Alicorn Meditation.

Mindful Acknowledgment

One of the most important pieces to noticing in a mindful way is to capture your unicorn moments in an active way. Active acknowledgment has a domino effect. The energy knows it's being received, so it continues to connect with you in the future. Your mind also realizes this is something worth paying attention to and sets a radar to watch for similar instances in the future.

Here are some things you can do to actively acknowledge your unicorn moments:

- Write them down.
- Keep a record of all your unicorn encounters that you can look back on.
- Create art inspired by the event.
- Take a picture or doodle a little sketch of whatever caught your attention.
- Keep a gratitude journal.

Do whatever works for you to confirm in your mind that something happened that you want to experience more of. Becoming mindful as a practice in your daily life will help you receive what you've been asking for. I carry notecards with me all the time, and sometimes I record notes in my phone or send emails to myself. It seems like unicorn moments never come at a convenient time. Like a dream, they soon fade and are forgotten, so recording them quickly can be a vital step in your practice.

The Little Things vs. the Big Things

So far we've focused on how distraction and a lack of focus can cause us to miss the magic in our lives. Another reason we might miss it is because we're only anticipating larger-than-life events and not paying attention to the smaller details. Understanding that there are different levels of unicorn encounters will help you recognize them, even when they are "just" little things.

What you consider to be a little or a big encounter is entirely objective, but both versions are important. The rarity of the big things, like catching sight of the northern lights or receiving a visitation dream, is easier to recognize because these events can be so shocking. A big encounter might be a sign of hope or inspiration you've been waiting for, even when you didn't consciously realize it. It causes you to do a double take and stop in your tracks. You might have goosebumps, feel a sense of amazement, and initially be confused, trying to process what you've just encountered or seen. If we miss these moments, it's usually because we choose not to believe in them. We clearly notice that they've occurred, but we disregard them anyway.

I experienced a big moment like this a few months after another surgery. I'd been healing but found my recovery to be a slow and serious business. While I was exuberant early on, in a kind of "post-exam" euphoria, the heavy side of it all took a firm hold as the weeks rolled by. Limitation, lack of exercise, and anxiety over lingering pain had all been taxing. Depression had become my unwelcome companion, and I was having trouble raising my head above it all. It was as though I'd been thrown into a midlife crisis of sorts. I wanted to throw out my life: my home, my job, my hobbies, my relationships. The desire to toss my life in the garbage and recreate myself was disorienting, especially during a time when I was physically bound. It felt like I was being asked to change while standing still.

I still looked for hope and happiness though. I

Unicorn moments soon fade and are forgotten, so recording them quickly can be a vital step.

was watching holiday movies on repeat in the middle of summer, being silly and dancing with my dog when the moment struck, and trying to find the lighter side of things. At one point I thought back to a clover plant that I'd bought earlier in the year when I decided to move forward with the surgery. Clover is a plant for luck, but within a month I'd killed it. I'd planned to put something else in the pot and moved it outdoors, but soon the clover reappeared without assistance and stronger than ever— the spirit of nature working magic behind the scenes. "Could that be me?" I wondered in my post-op phase. "Am I just in my withered moment?"

Then one morning in the flurry of another running-late morning, I let out a startled scream. Amid the neglected, weed-spotted landscaping (courtesy of all the physical limitations) was a single delicate pink rose. Just like I'd done with the clover, I'd sworn that rose bush was dead. I'd completely given up on her, but silently she'd worked her spell among the weeds. I didn't sense it dawning, yet suddenly it was there ... this beautiful thing that took me completely by surprise. Without help from anyone, she bloomed anyway, a unicorn right outside my window.

I hadn't had any other roses bloom that year, so that moment was definitely one that surprised and sent a thrill through me. While a flower is a small thing, the moment felt very significant. Someone else might have seen it as a little thing or even not meaningful at all, but for me it was a big moment. It provided the hope I desperately needed and it stuck with me for a very long time.

But what about the little things? These are the smaller moments of gratitude that you might collect throughout your days. A beautiful, sunny spring day after a long winter, hearing from your best friend when you're feeling down, or someone holding the door for you when your arms are full of groceries might all carry a significant uplifting energy for you. While these may be little everyday things, they happen more frequently than the "big" moments and can add up to provide exponential benefits, so keep an eye out to acknowledge those moments too.

When thinking about little things versus big things, another thing to consider is that something that might have been a rare occurrence could eventually become something you bring into your everyday life. An example of this is a euphoric experience I had at a live concert and how I brought that energy into my daily life by joining a choir, playing piano, and listening to newfound and tried-

and-true music in my creative space. In this way, you can eventually embody that energy. Those once rare inspirations will be less shocking when you come across them because they're no longer a rare occurrence in your life. Even though magical moments will continue to inspire and energize you, they change in such a way that you may not recognize them as a big thing. Instead, these encounters become a little lapdog unicorn, something you find encouragement and comfort in every day. And congratulations when you achieve this, because embodying the unicorn spirit is our goal!

The Need to Believe

Belief is a vital ingredient in being awake to the magic in our lives. Here we'll look at how we can make sure we're seeing things for what they truly are. Through a review of beliefs we hold around our experience, ourselves, and others, we can help ensure we don't miss the magic.

Believe in Your Experience

Maybe the magic is coming to you as synchronicity, as imagery in meditation, or as a message from your spirit guide in a dream. It can be really easy to dismiss these experiences, saying to yourself that you're being ridiculous. No matter how uplifting the experience may have been, logic tries to take over. This is especially the case because logic is what society currently values most. But if we disregard our authentic energetic experiences because it's not considered logical, then we're left always seeing the horse and never the unicorn. If we allow ourselves to believe, we add another magical layer to life that can be just as valuable.

I'm not saying that we need to throw logic out the window and believe everything without question. In fact, I'm a constant doubter. I often demand that my experiences prove themselves to me. For example, I've studied and practiced energy therapies for years and have both received and given sessions. (You'll get the chance to try energy work in the next chapter.) When I go through long stretches of not giving or receiving these sessions, my mind begins to doubt their reality. "That can't be real," I start to think. But the next time I'm part of the experience, I'm always left fully convinced of its merits once again. This is because I'm not just thinking about it in my mind, and I'm not just reading or hearing about it from someone else. I'm right there in it, feeling the energy, deep relaxation, and emotional or physical shifts that come about from it.

I could still cast that off as a false experience, telling myself I'm making it all up in my head. In the past there were times when I did just that. But I've returned to energy work enough times now that it's consistently proven itself to me. Even though I don't fully understand how it all works, I believe.

Honor your experience. Don't blindly dismiss it. Instead, sit with it and let it reveal its truth to you. If you're left unsure, ask for and seek out additional experiences that might help confirm it further.

Believe in Yourself

For my birthday one year, my siblings gave me a poster that I absolutely love. On it is an image of a unicorn lying on its back on a couch. Its legs are curled almost into the fetal position and its eyes are bugging out as a therapist sits looking on, saying nonchalantly, "You need to believe in yourself." This humorous and quirky inspiration shares some very grounded truth.

We all carry so much wisdom within us. It's in our physical body all the way down to the coding in our DNA and includes ancestral knowledge, wisdom that has been passed down to us from previous generations. It's also in our energy body as wisdom we ourselves have carried along with us into this life. Consider this a parallel to our physical genetic memory, but instead of coming from our ancestors, it's a code or stamp from the universe. Basically, in various ways we know things even when we might not understand why or how we know them. Part of being awake to the magic is learning to trust and believe in this internal wisdom.

For example, when I was all of six years old, my family and I were living in the basement of a new house we were building. Since our previous house had already sold, we'd packed up and made the cement world our little home for a time. While we had all the normal furnishings, sometimes it still felt scary to be in that space. Unfinished basements just have that vibe.

One day I was in the basement with a friend who was feeling scared, and I remember sharing a technique with her that I had used to help soothe myself. I was never taught this exercise. It was just something I started doing on my own at night when I got scared in bed.

"Imagine there's a bubble around you," I said to my friend. "It will protect you. Nothing bad can get in. Just pretend it's all full of light and you'll be so safe."

I'd completely forgotten that this was something I used to do until I started taking energy healing classes as an adult. When we were learning about the subtle energy body and protecting the aura, it all came flashing back to me. I couldn't believe the intuition I had about subtle energy as a kid. What else did I know then that I now have simply forgotten or tend to dismiss as an adult?

Once I made this realization, I started trusting more of the intuitive information I felt and received during energy healing sessions, intuitive readings, and meditation and throughout my days in general.

• EXERCISE 13 •

Learning to Trust Your Inner Wisdom

It's worthwhile to pay attention to whether or not you trust your own intuition. Trusting your inner wisdom means you listen to and honor your inner voice, whether it's your inner child or higher wise self. You allow yourself to follow your wants and desires as guides to finding your glitter. If you aren't quite sure whether this is something you're doing, try this exercise to help you connect with your inner wisdom.

As you've done before, find a quiet space and settle into a comfortable position. Take some calming breaths. When you feel ready, imagine that you're in a favorite meditation space. Maybe this is a warm beach where you can feel the sun on your skin and listen to the waves moving in and out on the sand. For me, it's a clearing in the middle of the woods with a trickling stream and a single large oak tree in the middle of the field. I walk from the edge of the woods to cross the stream and sit under the tree in its shade. For a while I'll listen to the water running over rocks, the wind moving through tall grass, and the birds that swoop through the branches overhead and up to the blue sky.

Find your calm space and let yourself experience it for a while. After a bit, notice a figure walking toward you. There's a welcoming smile on their face. You notice that something is familiar about them, but it's not clear what. Even though you can't quite place them, you're excited that they're there and you give them a hug. You sit together in your calming space, and they pull a small container out of their pocket. Maybe it's a wooden box, a locket, or an envelope. It shimmers as they hand it to you, and you take it in your hands. They ask you to open it and tell you it contains your inner wisdom. Take time to savor the message that's revealed. Make a mental note of the sights, sounds, feelings, and other sensory messages that come to you.

After you receive your inner wisdom, you close the container and hand it back to your companion. They take it back, and it's then that you realize this figure looks exactly like you. They are your inner guide. Before the two of you part, they remind you that you can call on them any time.

When your meditation is complete, slowly come back to your physical space. Write down what you experienced and the inner wisdom that came to you. Even if you don't understand it, it might be something that will become clearer in the future. As with the previous mindfulness practice, the more we call on and listen to our inner wisdom, the more it will make itself known. As with any relationship, the more we engage with our inner wisdom, the easier it will be to trust it.

Believe in Others

In chapter 2, we talked about our unicorn people. Think back to who these individuals are for you. Find those you're inspired by, not to worship or idolize them but to ignite kinetic energy within yourself. Belief here is about being motivated by your inspirations. You believe this person is amazing! What about them is so incredible? How can you embody that kind of sparkle?

Helping others rise to their potential and achieve their dreams is another form of believing in others. Look outside your own goals and think about how you can support others in the ways that you also wish to be (or have been) supported. Maybe this is by helping to tutor someone so they can achieve their academic goals, or perhaps you will sponsor or make a donation to someone's Kickstarter or entrepreneurial project. It could be as simple as putting up a kid's drawing on your refrigerator. In these ways, we keep each other moving by showing that we believe in each other's magical potential.

Clearing the Way to See

Magic exists right in your midst, yet it may be hidden under layers of mediocrity. Clearing clutter can be a catalyst for being able to clearly see yourself, your goals, and where you find joy. This practice can be a beacon that shines a light on what it is that you really want to be paying attention to.

Things like social clutter, creating relationship boundaries, and mental decluttering can be very challenging. The need for mental decluttering is more prominent now than ever before. With the constant barrage of technology, news, and work that we have to deal with, our stress and anxiety levels are at an all-time high.

Taking breaks from social media, technology, work, and life tasks can help you reset and allow your mind to rest. Having a regular stress-relief practice of some sort can also be very helpful. This could be a meditation practice, yoga, getting out on the river in your kayak, taking a walk with your dog, writing in your journal, or talking with your therapist. Whatever it is, this activity allows your mind to take a break from being "on" so that you can relax and let go. When we ensure that we're surrounded by healthy relationships and support our minds to be more at ease, we're more able to take notice of the positives in our lives.

While establishing relationship boundaries and mental decluttering are also important, we'll mainly be looking at clearing clutter in our living space, because our physical space is usually a reflection of the other two. By attending to our

Clearing clutter can be a catalyst for being able to clearly see yourself, your goals, and where you find joy.

environmental clutter, the confusion and disorder in other areas of our lives tends to magically follow suit. And if not, it at least becomes clearer what steps need to be taken to address them as well.

Decluttering Your Environment

For a few years I had a recurring dream that I simply couldn't figure out. I can now see that this dream was yet another type of unicorn dream for me, leading me to what I most desired and what would bring me authentic joy. In this particular dream I would always stumble upon a huge part of my home. The space was always something that I'd forgotten about or never even knew was there. I was always left wondering how I could have *possibly* forgotten it existed. There were large domed chambers made of marble and endless rooms filled with colorful fabrics, furniture, and art.

There's a place known as the "House on the Rock" in Spring Green, Wisconsin, that's reminiscent of the space I found myself in. The building is a fantastical and somewhat ridiculous place of unending rooms, architectural feats, and an enormous collection of knickknacks and random odd items. It includes a carousel room with angels hovering hauntingly above, and an infinity room that extends in a free float two hundred feet past the edge of a cliff. It is eccentric, peculiar, a little bit terrifying, and most definitely imaginative.

Sometimes in this recurring dream I was amazed to realize that *this space was all mine.* How could the previous owners have left it? How was I so lucky to own it? *How was I ever going to get it in order?* My mind would quickly jump from excitement to mortification that I hadn't remembered the space was available to me and complete overwhelm over not knowing what to do with it. The incredible potential of the space was so overwhelming that I would freeze before I could even get started.

In other versions of this dream, I would go into enormous and overwhelming antique stores that were stocked so full I could barely move. In the antique-store version of this dream, I was always extremely excited, even though I was overwhelmed. I knew that if I focused and was attentive to each individual item, I could discover all the pieces that were treasures. My special things were waiting to be found amid all the clutter.

Looking back now, the meaning of these dreams is incredibly obvious, but for a long time I just didn't get it. The unicorns didn't give up. The dreams kept coming until finally one day it clicked for me. It wasn't until I started decluttering my house that I realized the dreams were about my creative studio.

I'd lived in my home for five years, and I never felt like that area had come together in a way that made me want to spend time in it. I knew there was potential for it to be a beautiful, comfortable, and inspiring place; I just wasn't able to get it to that point. I also felt unfocused about what it was that I wanted to do creatively. I kept dabbling, buying and saving ingredients that didn't end up getting used and just added to the mess. There were totes crammed with fabric and toolboxes filled with drawing utensils, embroidery thread, needles, glass beads, and other jewelry-making items. A broken sewing machine sat unused. A button-making kit, purses, markers, paints, and more took up space. Aside from that, I had endless ideas of things I wanted to write and make. Sometimes I would try to follow through, but things always fell short and were eventually abandoned. Most often I stopped before I even began.

My surroundings matched the unfocused nature of my creative endeavors, and I was finally ready to clear things out on both levels. Down went the gallery wall of pictures and other odd items I'd mixed and matched. In its place I hung a single painting that I'd done years before.

Immediately things felt better. It was less busy, calmer, and there was already a better sense of focused intention.

The next task was to acquire something I'd wanted for years: a dresser. I'd held myself back from this because I already had a functional table, but it didn't fit my preferred shabby chic style. Looking at it left me uninspired and feeling like I was in a garage. I'd always told myself it served a purpose and so was good enough, but in fact it was not serving the kind of function I needed. With so many odds and ends, I needed *drawers*. It was time to let the table go.

I was able to sell the table and use the money to purchase an old dresser in my favorite vintage style. After some paint and cleanup, it was perfect. I ditched all the toolboxes for drawer space. This opened up cupboard space where I could put the fabric I'd previously jammed into all the totes that had been taking up lots of room. These totes held random pieces of cloth and fabric that I'd been collecting for almost twenty years *just in case*. I thinned it all out, and by letting go of a plethora of unneeded and unused items, I was able to display my kept fabrics so that they became a stored resource while also being decorative display on the shelves. This added immensely to the positive feel of the space. Seeing things in this way had me wanting to break out my paintbrushes and get creating!

Decluttering can be a pain in the ass, but it can also be extremely liberating. Now, instead of diving into bins and hoping I come out with something I can use, I know I can use every piece of fabric I've kept. As a bonus, I'm able to find exactly what I need when I need it. And this is just one little example. As I cleared things out, one thing after another made sense. "Why do I have this?" I would ask myself. "That's not the kind of art I want to make. I'll never use this thing." As I let go, I better understood the purpose for the items that I desired to keep, and my creative inspirations grew.

• EXERCISE 14 •
Decluttering Your Environment

Now it's your turn. Decluttering your space might sound completely overwhelming. We gradually take on so much stuff and are good at cramming a lot of things into our spaces. The best strategy I've found is to create a priority list and make a schedule. It might look something like this:

- *June:* bedrooms and bedroom closets
- *July:* bathrooms

- *August:* living room, dining room, and bookshelves
- *September:* entry closet
- *October:* entertainment center and kitchen pantry
- *November:* kitchen
- *December:* storage totes and holiday decorations
- *January:* computer files
- *February:* CD binders and photo albums
- *March:* filing cabinet
- *April:* creative space
- *May:* garage

This is a list that I started a couple of years ago. I was extremely motivated, but the project was put on hold for a time due to health issues. Eventually I got back to it. Even though I fell off schedule, having the list helped me map out my space and prioritize the smaller pieces of the overall goal. Because of this, when I stopped for a while, I knew I wasn't giving up on it. I still felt inspired to come back to it whenever I could. Looking at this list made what previously felt insurmountable feel attainable instead.

Starting with the bedroom and bathroom is the easiest because we tend to jam our closets with things we don't really need or want. Diving in here can set a good pace and get you into a rhythm of letting go of things. I also aligned the list to significant dates. I knew I would already be going through holiday totes in December and the filing cabinet for taxes in April, so that's when I scheduled those areas to be decluttered. I knew I would have more patience for things like computer files, CD binders, and photos when I was hunkered down for the winter. Those nitty-gritty items are usually better to sort toward the end of the process since you'll probably be finding stray CDs, flash drives, photos, and papers for filing as you go through all the other areas of your living space.

Once you have the larger pieces of your schedule mapped out, you can break down each section even further if you wish. For example, for the kitchen you might set a goal to finish going through a certain amount of cupboard space each day or week, your refrigerator on a specific day, and so on. As you dive into things, try not to think of the larger goal or you might get overwhelmed. Instead, remember your mindfulness practice and just take it one room and one drawer at a time.

Throughout the process of decluttering, sort your unwanted items into the following groups:

- To repair (and eventually keep, donate, gift, or sell)
- To donate
- To gift (There's a "free table" at my workplace that is awesome for this.)
- To sell
- To recycle or throw away

Try to get your unwanted things in the hands of people who will really make use of them. Books are meant to be read. Tools are meant to be used. Furniture should be functional. Clothes should be worn, not hidden away in a dark closet. I had a sewing machine I never used because I could never get the tension to work properly, but I held onto it for years because *I wanted a sewing machine*. But it wasn't any good to me if I couldn't get it to work properly. I didn't want to throw it away, but I also didn't want to donate it and cause the same issue for someone else. Finally, I listed it for free online and included a note about the tension problem. Someone picked it up and didn't care at all about the issue. Now it's serving its purpose and was saved from going in the garbage, and I created space for me to get a machine that I love and am actually able to make use of.

★ ★ ★

As decluttering gurus like Tisha Morris and Marie Kondo say, your things should reflect who you are now, not who you used to be. Of course, if a part of you still carries a great love for something you liked in the past, then maybe that's still who you are now and it's okay to hold onto it.

I still have a couple of Rainbow Brite videotapes that I keep in my creative studio. I can't watch the tapes anymore since I don't have a working Beta player, but the art on the cases makes me really happy. When I open a case and hold the tape, I'm transported to the home of my early childhood and cozy time with my big sister. It warms my heart and so is still a meaningful item for me to hold onto.

If something is a reminder of the things you used to love and still love in the present time, by all means hold onto it. I always keep one tote of keepsakes. I go through it once a year to be reminded of good memories, and sometimes I find that I finally feel ready to get rid of certain items.

Decluttering is a learned skill. It's one I've gotten really good at because clutter totally stresses me out, but it's taken me a long time to learn how to do it. If you still have a hard time letting go of things, check the recommended resources at the end of this book for more inspiration and guidance.

Making room for new energy is the real fun and reward of the decluttering process. By letting go of what's been blocking you, you'll be able to clearly see what it is that you actually want. It's almost magical. The cherry on top for me in the earlier example was something I'd been really desiring but hadn't been able to figure out before. When I bought my house and before I was even in it, I swore I would have a chandelier somewhere.

I just didn't know where. More than five years later, I remained chandelier-less, but while I was setting up my creative studio, inspiration hit me. This was where it needed to be! For some reason I couldn't see that before. Yet now that I was moving energy all around, it was crystal clear. I could finally understand the space, and this was where I wanted to glitter and shine.

I purchased a chandelier soon after, and Luke surprised me and hung it up while I was out one evening. When I walked in, I shouted in surprise. I was totally giddy when I saw it. It was so freakin' perfect. Shiny! Sparkly! It made the room glow. Even though it was the middle of summer, for the rest of the night I had "Silver and Gold" from *Rudolph the Red-Nosed Reindeer* stuck in my head. I repeatedly went back to the space just to stare at the bejeweled light. Not long after that, I settled into the space and started writing this book.

When we let go, we create space to draw in what we most want to create in our lives.

★ ★ ★

You've started clearing your space and are learning to believe, and it's all adding to your ability to attune to the magic all around you. You're well on your way now! Let's take it to the next level and get into the finer details of where exactly your personal vibrance lives.

chapter four

Chapter Five

FINDING WHAT MAKES YOU SPARKLE

As you've been learning about the tools of the unicorn and ways to ensure you're more awake to the magic, hopefully you've had some insights into the things that make you shine from the inside out. If you're feeling unsure, returning to the source of your sparkle will help you remember what brings you joy. We touched on some of this earlier in our discussion of forgotten passions and hidden personality quirks in chapter 2, but we'll take another look here so you have even more specific guidance on finding what lights you up.

Being playful and finding hidden truths about ourselves is important, but it's not just about joy. The unicorn horn is said to purify all that it touches. These beings are like light that walks into the darkness, asking it to harmonize with them and rise to their level. We will also look into the darkness and try to bring it into the light. Part of this discussion will focus on unicorn energy as seen through the chakras and how we can go about polishing our sparkle so it shines even brighter.

Returning to the Source of Your Sparkle

When I came across the notion of trying to find what lights us up so that we can feel our spirit, I was honestly at a loss for what that might be for me. My first thought was that it must be books and art, but those things were already part of my life and I still felt I was missing something. I thought I must be so immersed in those worlds as jobs that I was just not able to see or recognize the sparkle in it anymore. This left me feeling disheartened, but I still kept my ears open, listening for whatever might bring out an extra spark. A deeper part of me knew that if

I was truly shining with all the light I had, I wouldn't feel this sense of incompleteness or lack.

Later that year I went to a concert with a friend and felt positively buoyant, as though my energy was expanding in all directions, my aura reaching out to meet all four walls of the room, trying to drink in the notes hanging in the air. I couldn't stop smiling. It lit me up. As a fairly reserved person, I found myself uncharacteristically dancing, singing along, and shouting out to the band in exclamation. I simply couldn't hold my good vibes back, nor should I have. I was euphoric, in great company, and thought to myself, "I need more of this in my life."

This was a clear sparkle moment. I realized music was one of my unicorn tools. It was something I'd enjoyed a lot as a teenager, but in the serious actions of becoming a self-sufficient adult (school, finances, debt, job, health challenges, etc.), I'd let it go. Looking back, I realized that theater was something I'd enjoyed just as much. It was something that energized me and sent positive vibrations through every part of me.

After these realizations, I started gradually and somewhat unconsciously reincorporating this rediscovered unicorn tool into my life. I dug out CDs and records

I'd listened to as a kid and also started listening to more musical soundtracks. I created a designated space where I more consistently listened to music, leaving the TV behind. I spent time playing piano, very badly, but that didn't matter; it still made my energy sing. I joined a choir and looked into free summer concerts in the park that I could attend. I bought tickets to a concert for someone I'd really wanted to see perform more than a decade earlier. Normally I would have once again told myself that I shouldn't go, but more and more I was recognizing the importance of feeding this passion. I decided I would go to at least once concert or musical a year. I could certainly manage that, and the decision solidified the fact that I was making this rediscovered passion a priority.

These changes weren't forced and didn't need to be overly thought out or preplanned, but there was a certain level of intention for seeking them out to create more music in my life. And it was making a difference. In addition to music, I started finding new ways to approach books and art, two areas I knew I had lots of passion for that just needed to be reignited. Since they had become very work-focused areas of my life, my mind perceived them as serious business, so my spirit paid them less attention. To get out of that mindset and rediscover my sparkle, I turned to reading books in my spare time that were the opposite of my professional focus. Instead of nonfiction wellness, I started reading children's classics, illustrated poetry books, and graphic novels, which served my love of books and art all at once.

• EXERCISE 15 •
What's Blocking You?

There will be obstacles in your way as you're trying to return to the source of your sparkle. As you're trying to hunt down light, also be on the lookout for the things that are getting in the way. Think about what you're spending your time and attention on. There is probably something you're currently doing that doesn't really inspire you, and it might even be something you despise. Guilt-ridden obligations, time-sucks, trying to please others, and putting others' needs above your own all fit this list.

Sometimes we need to do things that don't totally inspire us, and it can still be okay because we have some level of balance with it. But when that thing is soul-crushing and a vampire drain on your energy that provides no benefit, or when the benefit doesn't feel worth the cost, it's time to look at how you can let go of that circumstance and replace it with the things that feed you.

One example for me is TV addiction. I fully admit to this addiction. I love TV. I have spent entire days doing nothing but watching it. Every day I watch at least an hour, which I think is pretty normal, but too many days I come home from work, plop down on the couch, and do pretty much nothing else for the rest of the evening. There are times when I just allow myself to revel in it, but when it came to a point where I was getting frustrated over not achieving my life goals, I eventually determined that this addiction was hindering me and needed some boundaries. In order to curb it, I try to designate at least a portion of my evening to non-screen-time reading, looking at or creating art, writing, listening to music, putting together a puzzle, doing chores (not fun, but a clean house makes me super happy), or doing any number of other things that feed me.

There's a cost and a benefit that we are always trying to balance in our lives. Your job that you don't really like might be providing vital financial support that you haven't been able to find anywhere else. You might be a caretaker to a loved one

who leaves you feeling exhausted, but an underlying love sustains the task. In some cases we may just need extra support from others to help us continue on with our current situation but in a way that allows us to feed ourselves on the side. If caretaking is your constant focus but it's leaving you sad, angry, depressed, and spent, with nothing left for yourself, then getting support so you can go to a weekly choir session or get a massage or attend to whatever your sparkle is all about will be vital in helping you build yourself back up.

Now it's your turn. What is your number-one addiction or obstacle that's holding you back? Or expand from there and write out a list of your top blocks. Think about what you can do to counter these things so they no longer are a hindrance to finding what makes you sparkle.

Being Playful

Imagine you're a plant that needs regular water and sunshine to survive. Your water is what you get from shelter, food, and all the practical details of survival. The sunshine is the sparkling magic. How do you make sure you're placing yourself in the sun?

As I mentioned before, books and art became less of a sparkle for me and more of an everyday job—the water for my survival. I needed to reawaken my sense of play to breathe new life into it all. Instead of focusing all my creative energy on achieving a sellable or perfect final product, I played with paint-by-number kits and seek-and-find books like *Where's Waldo?* Instead of reading adult books, I turned to more playful options. A personal favorite of mine is the Phoebe and Her Unicorn comic series, which features a unicorn as the main character. These books are silly and fun and remind me of my childlike nature.

This playfulness is a piece of myself that I grew unattached to early on and have sought to return to. I can remember even at a young age playing with friends who wanted to play dress-up or play house and feeling absolutely ridiculous. I wanted to be in their world, but I was self-conscious. I felt like I wasn't doing it right and had the sense that I was just too old, even though I definitely was not. I would ask for a stuffed animal for Christmas or a doll for my birthday, but then feel utterly absurd once I received it. There was a longing to play, but practicality had taken over and I'd lost the ability.

Part of rediscovering how to play means getting over the fear of being seen as silly. Once I started taking hold of the things that brought me back to life, the new focus developed its own momentum and showed up in other expressive ways, to the point where sometimes I couldn't stop even when I sort of wanted to. I remember one time with my brother when I was being especially silly, singing my thoughts in the way of Jess Day from *New Girl*. "Sorry, I can't help but be me," I said, apologizing for the fact that I was probably being annoying.

"Good," he replied with a laugh and a smile. I never felt more acknowledged in my life.

Whatever these playful things may be for you, they should be things that get you really excited and breathe new life into the everyday humdrum. They also usually aren't about an end result or product. Instead, they get you really in the moment only for the purpose of that moment. Maybe it's flying a kite or dusting off your bike and getting into some nature trails. Maybe you've always wanted to learn how to knit or learn a different language. Or maybe you used to play basketball as a kid and you realize it's actually something that you've really been missing.

Ideally, you'll be able to find some things that can be done somewhat regularly. A day at the water park could be thrilling and filled with play. If that's what you want to do for fun, great! Go out and do it. But also find something you can do weekly or even daily to feed your sense of fun and play. This could lead to bigger things, but that's not the initial goal. If you feel excited and energized by the idea of writing one poem every day, good! Be in those moments of writing each poem for the purpose of expression, play, and engagement with your own creative self. If, in the end, you find yourself compiling your playful endeavors into a book, hooray! But the key here is that we are relearning how to cultivate fun and playfulness for its own sake instead of for an end goal or achievement. This is because culturally we're trained to act for the purpose of production and results. While goals can be important and inspiring, for now that's not where we're setting our focus.

Where Is Your Sparkle Stuck?

As you're trying to discover your playful side, it can also be really helpful to dig into where your sparkle might be stuck. Often there's a key time period that we can pin down as being significant. This is often when you let go of doing things that you used to really enjoy. Like a time machine, you can go back to reclaim it and bring it into your present. Since childhood was where I left my sparkle (very common), that was mainly where I went to search for my lost treasures.

Finding where our sparkle is stuck can be really hard to pin down at first because we've convinced ourselves that we don't need these parts of ourselves, even though they're usually the things that bring us the most joy. We do a very good job of hypnotizing ourselves to that. In order to remedy what's been lost, we need to pay attention to what we gravitate toward. Often these are things that we don't let ourselves have or do. Clues to where our sparkle is stuck include:

- Gifts we give
- Things we find nostalgic
- Our wants and desires

One clue to figuring out this mystery is to look at the gifts you give to others, whether those are physical things, events, gifts of time, or something else. We literally give away what we love most. We think we can't enjoy it ourselves, and we figure, if not us, then *someone* should be able to enjoy it. So we gift it away.

Nostalgia can also act as a compass guiding you toward the things that make you light up. When I became wise to this, I explained it to Luke so that I could start embracing this childhood part of myself without feeling weird about it. Okay, I still felt a bit weird, but at least I knew he understood. During this time, I watched a ton of cartoons. I started a Pinterest board that I named "80s Kid at Heart" and pinned all the things that hit me sentimentally when I saw them. There was an emotional connection to things I'd played, watched, and enjoyed as a kid. I remembered that I'd really loved Garfield, so I started reading the comic strip every day. At one point, Luke joined in and bought me a stuffed animal of Pinkie Pie, a favored character from My Little Pony. I'd latched onto her because she was so silly, fun, and quirky, all qualities I was trying to find more of in myself. I carried her around solidly for a couple of years and still bring her out for an extra sense of security when I'm feeling under the weather.

It might seem silly and embarrassing, but in order to get your sparkle out from where it first became stuffed away, you need to embrace the feeling of where you were when it was lost. Fully own that lost happiness in whatever way you can, and it will eventually become yours again. Trust your wants and desires as guides to finding your glitter.

★ ★ ★

Finding Where Your Sparkle Is Stuck

Finding where our sparkle is stuck can be really hard to pin down at first because we've convinced ourselves that we don't need these parts of ourselves, even though they're usually the things that bring us the most joy. Clues to where our sparkle is stuck include:

- Gifts we give
- Things we find nostalgic
- Our wants and desires

• EXERCISE 16 •
Mindfulness for Finding Where Your Sparkle Is Stuck

There are different things you can do to help uncover your own path to finding your playful side and also to discover at what point in life your sparkle might have become buried. Here are a couple of ideas in the form of keeping lists:

- Start keeping a list of things you gift to others. See if there are any hints there as to what you yourself would really enjoy. Maybe it's puzzles, coloring books, board games, flowers, painting sets, sports equipment, kitchen tools, or something completely different.

- Write out a list of things you did as a kid that you especially loved. Or if your childhood wasn't particularly a highlight of your life, do this for whatever point in time you feel most drawn to in the form of nostalgia. Keep the list handy and add to it as you recall things that you'd forgotten all about. To help jog your memory, go through old photos, start a board on Pinterest like I did, or go through magazines and collect images of things that you loved. One thing will lead to another and another until eventually you form a more complete picture. From this list, what is at least one thing you would be excited to pick up again?

Adding Extra Glitter

Hopefully by now you have some idea of what will bring back or heighten your sparkle and sense of play. If you're still feeling stuck and can't hear your internal guidance on where to go from here, below are some additional ideas that may be helpful. These are all things that can increase our levels of happiness (McAllister 2018). See what stands out to you most and go with it. It may lead you to just the thing you're looking for.

- Having meaningful activity. This is something that gets you up and about. It could be a job, a hobby, volunteering, etc.
- Spending time with animals
- Engaging in creative activity
- Social connection and community

- Getting out in nature
- Acts of kindness and caring for others
- Consciously looking for beauty as you go about your days
- Some sort of faith practice or spiritual belief. This doesn't automatically mean religion or church. It could be music, nature, meditation, or some other practice that helps you feel spiritually connected or part of a greater whole.
- Whatever fills you with a sense of purpose or meaningful direction. This is something that leaves you feeling like you're contributing to the world in some way. It could be the role you play in your family, your job, a hobby, volunteer work, or something completely different. Maybe you plant a tree every day or pick up litter whenever you take a walk, leaving you feeling like you are leaving the earth in a better state than it would have been without you.

- Seeking out pleasurable and fun activities in a very intentional way. Maybe it's hitting new state parks to go hiking, deciding to go to at least one concert a year (and having that to look forward to), signing up for a community education class in something you've always wanted to learn how to do, or watching for events that pop up in your community, like outdoor concerts, car shows, and art fairs. In short, you aren't waiting around for fun to happen. You're looking and planning for it.

- Finding flexibility with change, transition, and your current circumstances. Sometimes this can be extremely challenging, but if we're able to roll with the punches, we're also able to more easily let go of glitter items that are no longer a good fit for us. By letting go, we can then find new things that better fit our current condition.

It's Not Just About Joy

A lot of what we've looked at with unicorns so far has to do with the positives, but they also show us how to approach the darker aspects of life. It may seem counter-intuitive, but looking into the darkness is also important along our journey toward finding the things that make us shine. The seemingly contradictory characteristics that unicorns have show a mastery of balance and honoring the self. Who else can be noble and wise while also allowing an expression of vanity and ego to such a strong degree? In this way, they who us how to honor all of our supposed imperfections as well.

Unicorns are light that doesn't shrink away from the dark. They're a reflection of our potential to rise to higher levels, even when we carry our shadow side along with us. Whether we're dealing with healing wounds from childhood, the trappings of our ego, challenges of mental or physical health, or some other shadow burden, unicorns remind us that we possess a natural internal balance. We may be able to find it on our own or we may need to seek the help of others who have a more objective view. Either way, hope is there.

For example, I used to have a recurring dream where I was choking. With no one coming to my rescue, I would shove my hand down my throat and grab onto whatever was blocking my airway to pull it out. Sometimes I would come up with tangled threads of plastic netting or dead matter that seemed to never end, but most often it was a long black snake. I would pull frantically until I awoke, breathless and gasping for air. It wasn't until I brought this up to a doctor that I gained insight into why I kept having this dream.

"Where do you feel this dream in your body?" I was asked.

I felt into the dream, pinpointing the exact spot. "It's deep in the back of my throat."

She paused for a second and then asked, "Do you feel you have any grief that you haven't processed?"

Without time to even think about the question, I burst into tears. Soon after, I started therapy and began unpacking sadness that spanned my entire lifetime, even back to trauma from a premature birth. Soon after therapy began, the choking dreams stopped. I'd gotten the message and was addressing it to heal myself and recover buried happiness, so the dreams were no longer needed.

Working with unicorn energy isn't just about the fluffy niceness of cheerfulness and bliss. I would never claim that joy is something that's always easily found, because often it's *not*. Thinking positive thoughts in order to achieve happiness has a place, but finding authentic happiness usually isn't as easy as that. Unicorns are *elusive*. They evade sight and capture. They hide, disguise themselves, or are simply not recognized when they're seen. Meeting the challenge to seek and find them anyway is what we've been addressing in this book. By now you probably see this usually takes some active effort on our part.

It can be easy to assume that if happiness doesn't come easily, then it must not be meant for you. This illusion is due in part to the sense of isolation that darkness causes. It might look like everyone around you is floating on easy clouds while you're struggling to keep your head above murky waves, but sometimes we actually have to go into and touch the darkness in order to real-

Unicorns are a reflection of our potential to rise to higher levels, even when we carry our shadow side along with us.

ize our own joy. If you're in the darkness and what I'm saying sounds impossible or like hollow words, know that I've been there too.

The rose story I told earlier is an example of this. I was in a dark space, yet I was still able to acknowledge a magical moment and the message it held for me. I was deep in the space of my shadow side, fully reflecting on every aspect of my life and ready to throw it all out the window. There were a lot of unhappy thoughts and sob sessions. I didn't shy away from it. I felt it. I talked through it. I wrote about it and followed creative expression as a therapeutic balm. It was not a sugar-coated time, but I was still able to acknowledge some of the beauty that broke through to me as the shock of a unicorn encounter. And I was still able to hope for more. While these moments may not save us by totally fixing the circumstances, if we let them, they can become one more lead to guide us out of the dark.

Earlier we talked about how we might miss unicorn moments due to distraction and how practicing mindfulness can help with this. Another reason that we might let unicorns pass us by is because the challenges we face cause us to keep our head down in an attempt to push through. In this state, we don't recognize them for what they are when they finally do appear. Instead of a unicorn, we see a horse or even nothing at all. When life becomes serious business and a problem whose solution we're in constant pursuit of, light has a harder time winding its way through the cracks to get to us. If it does finally reach us, we might repeatedly disbelieve our unicorns and dismiss them as not good enough since whatever they bring may not be the direct answer to the problem we've been trying to solve.

Yet another possibility is that we recognize the unicorn but don't trust it. You might have experienced the loss of joy in the past and now believe it can't last. You might be afraid to let yourself experience the vibrant highs of life, assuming that the pain of the eventual fall won't be worth it.

To move through these shadow beliefs, we need to rebuild trust in ourselves, others, and life itself. Some of the things we've talked about in this chapter might help you move through the dark challenges you face. For example, allowing yourself to play might be one glimmer of light that turns into a great support. If you need even more support, it can be immensely helpful to talk with a friend, loved one, or professional therapist to help get through the dark.

Polishing the Sparkle

So far in this chapter, we've looked at how actively seeking things that make us light up and bring back our playful side can create a cascade of positive energy and lead to additional goodness in our lives. We've also addressed how walking directly into our shadow spaces can be an important and sometimes unavoidable step on our journey. Whether we journal on our own, seek out others such as a therapist, or process in other ways, this challenging work of facing loss, disbelief, a sense of defeat, a lack of trust, or our basic fears can bring us to a whole new level.

We're going to follow up the challenging topic of shadow work with a practice that you can use to help polish your sparkle. Think of this as your energetic decluttering exercise. Earlier you worked on clearing clutter and removing it from your physical space. Now that you've started shaking things up on an emotional and mental level, this practice will help clear the cobwebs out of your personal vibrational space.

Your Energy Body

Before we dive into the actual practice, it's helpful to have a basic understanding of the subtle energy body. We all have a physical body that's easy to comprehend. Science has laid out and identified our organs and body systems and their basic functions. But on an energetic level, we also have a body that is difficult but not impossible to see. Many psychics and energy medicine practitioners are able to see the subtle body with their physical eyes or envision it in their mind's eye to gather health insights and information.

Our understanding of the subtle body carries ancient and sacred wisdom that has been handed down for thousands of years. Logically and scientifically, our understanding of these systems is still evolving. For example, in Traditional Chinese Medicine, it's taught that we have different meridian lines through which vital life energy flows and moves around the body. This concept is utilized in a variety of healing methods, from reflexology and acupuncture to chi gong, yoga, and massage. Yet the existence of the meridian system wasn't scientifically confirmed until 2016. There is so much yet to be discovered from a scientific point of view about ancient and intuited health wisdom, yet this wisdom continues to provide us with a compass direction along the way.

The Chakras

The pieces of your energy body that I want you to know about are the aura and the chakras. As a reminder, the chakras are the energy centers that run from your lower spine to the top of your head. If you need a reminder, you can go back to the chakra descriptions in chapter 2. So far we've focused mainly on the sixth chakra, but in the next exercise we'll be making use of all seven of them.

The Aura

The aura is the electromagnetic bubble that expands out around your body. It extends two to three feet around you, including above and below you. There are different layers to the aura, but for our purposes here, it's not important to get into those finer details. Just know that the aura can influence our various states of wellness, from emotional and mental to physical and spiritual health. It contains our own energy but can also collect the energy of others. For this reason, we'll be shaking loose some of the energy we're hanging onto that we don't need.

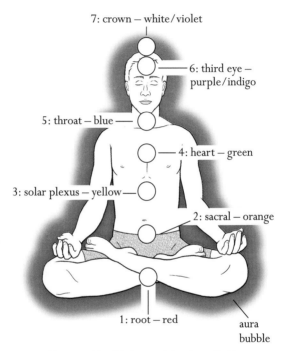

7: crown — white/violet

6: third eye —
purple/indigo

5: throat — blue —

4: heart — green

3: solar plexus — yellow—

2: sacral — orange

1: root — red

aura
bubble

Figure 2: The Chakras and the Auric Field

Chakras Through the Unicorn Lens

When you're shooting sunbeams from the sparkle in your eyes and have a toothy smile, unicorn energy is definitely there filling up your subtle energy body. Unicorns are strong and unafraid. This courage translates to chakras 1–4 to provide support and build up confidence. Unicorns also awaken our imagination, ask us to dream, and help us find our creative passions. In this way, they are intimately tied to chakras 4–7. But it's the heart, third eye, and crown chakras that unicorns harmonize most strongly with. We'll take a more detailed look at these chakra connections in the following exercise.

• EXERCISE 17 •
Unicorn Chakra Energy Clearing

This unicorn chakra energy clearing practice is intended to heal old wounds and shake off energy that's no longer serving you.

Preparation

Before you begin, if you have a photo of someone who is a unicorn person to you, place that in the space where you'll be doing this practice. Also gather your favorite crystals, especially the one that you identified earlier as your personal unicorn crystal. Spray some of your unicorn energy mist around the room. As you do, either repeat the intention that you connected to your mist or create a new intention specific to why you want to perform this exercise today.

Now that you've raised the energy around you, sit or lie down in whatever way is most comfortable for you. Breathe in and out, finding a slow and deep pace. Allow your muscles to relax. Let go, deeper and deeper. If you have trouble with this, try focusing on different body areas, from your feet to your calves to your knees and on up to your head, and with each piece, focus on relaxing that area. When you feel settled in, you can move on to the next step.

Welcoming the Unicorn

Your unicorn guide is going to be a partner for your practice. As you get comfortable, imagine that they're standing or lying quietly by your side. Allow them to appear to you. Notice the color of their coat and how their mane feels when you brush it with your hands. Rest your palm on the side of their face as a greeting and look into their eyes. Listen for the wisdom they have to share with you. Open yourself to feel the love that's radiating out and enfolding you. As you move through this practice, remember that your unicorn guide is guarding you and is ready to help you when needed.

Clearing the Aura

Now turn back to yourself. To begin, you're going to wipe your aura. Psychic and spiritual teacher Echo Bodine explains that as we go about our days, energy that we come into contact with can stick to our aura like static cling. To counter this, it's helpful to imagine running a giant lint roller over your aura. In your mind's eye, imagine that you see your personal energy. You might perceive foreign energy as cloudy areas, muddy colors, or specks within your aura. Envision the giant roller running from the top of your energy body down to your feet. Repeat this at different angles around your body until you've made it all the way around your energy bubble. If you still see energy that's not your own, repeat the process as many times as you'd like until it appears to be resolved and your aura is left shining.

If you have any remaining negative energy that you feel as anxious thoughts or discomfort in your body, focus on those now. Envision these negative sensations rising like steam, up and away from your body. Gather it all together like you're collecting bits of stray yarn. Scoop it up and roll it into a ball in your hands. Now extend your open palm and allow your unicorn guide to take the negativity from you.

Finding Courage in the Forest (Chakras 1–4)

Now that your aura has been attended to, we'll move on to the chakras. The first phase of your chakra work connects to chakras 1–4. These chakras help you find your courage in the forest. Focus in on your first chakra. See the bright ruby-red color glowing at the base of your spine. After you've connected with your root chakra for a bit, do the same for your second chakra, just below your navel. See the orange glow emanating from this space. Moving up, now envision a bright yellow sun beaming from the center of your stomach. And still higher, see an emerald glow expanding out from your open heart. Watch these lights dance and merge into one another as they grow. Feel warmth growing from the center and out from these spaces. Take some time to relax and enjoy the feeling and imagery that comes to you. When you feel ready, you can move on to the next step.

Finding Creativity in the Magical Realm (Chakras 4–7)

The second phase of your chakra work connects to chakras 4–7. These chakras help you find your creativity in the magical realm. Focus in again on your heart chakra (the bridge between the lower and the upper chakras), and see its emerald light reaching up toward your throat chakra. It acts as a switch and lights up the blue energy at your throat. Moving up, see the purple/indigo of your third eye shining like a beacon from your forehead. Finally, envision the brilliant white/violet energy at your crown beaming up toward the sky. Sit with these four chakras and see them shining together in harmony. Before you begin the next phase, take your unicorn crystal and place it over your heart, the bridge between the lower and the upper chakras.

Union and Balance with the Alicorn Spiral

Your chakras are all alight, and now we'll move on to harmonizing them. You can think of this step like finding the right keys on a keyboard for playing a chord, or setting off a clock pendulum that will align other pendulums to move in sync with it. Instead of a clock, I envision this as the more perceptible ring and sensation of a tuning fork. Instead of a tuning fork, your unicorn guide will provide the attunement for your energy to align with.

As you're sitting or lying down, your unicorn guide comes to stand over you. Their presence is strong and steady. They slowly bow their head to you in a sacred gesture of love and touch you on the crown with their spiraled alicorn.

Immediately, the energy from your crown chakra sparkles like glitter. It's as though a wick has been lit and the light travels down to your third eye, throat, heart, and so on. As the light reaches each energy center, it spits with extra light, like setting off mini-fireworks.

Once all seven chakras have been touched, the connected light begins to turn, moving the united energy from root to crown in a coiled pattern through the center of your body. Like nature's shells, flowers, DNA, weather patterns, and even the greater galax-

Unicorns awaken our imagination, ask us to dream, and help us find our creative passions.

ies, your subtle energy moves through the center of your body in a sacred spiral.

Sit with this step of the practice for as long as you'd like. It may be a couple of minutes or it may be a half hour, an hour, or more. If your mind wanders, bring it back to focus on the spiral movement running from your root and up and out from your crown. This intentional reconnection to the energy of the universe reminds every piece of you to trust and align with nature's wisdom for stability so that you can let go of the things that are not efficient or beneficial for you. It reminds you how to return to balance.

Closing

At the end of your practice, slowly bring yourself back to your physical space. Wiggle your fingers and toes. Open your eyes. Shake your arms and legs to get yourself back into your body and the physical space.

To close your practice, spray some of your unicorn mist onto your hands. Dab some of it to anoint your forehead for good thoughts, your throat for clear communication, and your heart to give and receive love. Finally, brush your hands through your aura, as though you were gently dusting yourself off, but away from your physical body within your aura. This helps to clear out any lingering energy that you've let go of.

Now take out your journal and write down anything you'd like to remember from your practice. List the things that you sensed. Also make a note of whether there was a main message that came to you and whatever your strongest takeaway was. Even if it's simply that you feel very relaxed, that is a positive effect worth noting. It's good to record your experience, because our memories of these kinds of moments tend to fade quickly, like dreams.

★ ★ ★

We've come a long way on this unicorn journey, from fable and ancient history to a personal practice and experience you can make your own. Unicorns are amazing guides in archetypal metaphor and as spirit guardians. In the next chapter, we'll take an even deeper look at how you can connect with unicorns through your own unique spiritual practice.

Chapter Six

CALLING IN
THE UNICORN

You've learned a lot so far about how to engage with unicorn energy and encourage it to inhabit your life in a more conscious way. In this chapter, we'll be looking even more deeply at how we can connect with this energy as a consistent and sacred practice. Psychic skills are another set of tools the unicorn uses. Having an understanding of these abilities as a form of spiritual "listening"

can be especially helpful as you move forward. But first, let's look at the different phases of calling in the unicorn.

Ask, Attract, Listen, Allow, and Receive

While sometimes our unicorn experiences are about hearing them when they are calling to us, other times it's about us calling out to them. There are several things that support calling in unicorn magic. These include:

- Ritual, prayer, mantra, affirmation (asking and attracting)
- Meditation (listening and allowing)
- Mindfulness (being awake and receiving)

We've gotten into that last item quite a bit already, but now we'll look at all of these pieces to show how they work together.

Ritual, Prayer, Mantra, and Affirmation (Asking and Attracting)

Ritual, prayer, mantra, and affirmation are all different ways you can put out your request in a positive and receptive way to help you attract a response. Maybe there's a version you're most drawn to. Defining each one a bit more should help you to decide.

Ritual is a form of sacred tradition that comes with certain steps. It can be anything from a church ceremony or a practice to mark a seasonal transition to the way you prepare for the day, practice yoga, or take a bath. The idea of a "sacred bath" may sound a bit odd, but it's really not. Without knowing it, we practice ritual quite often throughout our days. By making certain actions more intentional, we can take our practice to a ritual level. We can become more conscious of the call we're sending out, which also allows us to listen more intently for the response to our request.

Prayer can be a part of ritual or can be done all on its own. It's a form of asking that doesn't have to include kneeling, folding your hands, and speaking to a divine being, although that's certainly an option. It can be anything that brings you a sense of oneness or a feeling of being seen and heard. For you, this might mean being in nature, listening to music, writing in your journal, speaking with a friend or therapist, or any number of other activities. The key to prayer is that within it there is a sincere request for help and a feeling of trust and gratitude for being heard.

Your prayer might become a repeated mantra or affirmation. Mantras are words or sounds that are repeated for beneficial mental and spiritual effect. A very popular mantra is *Om*, a sound that represents the universe. Repeating this mantra (pronounced "aum," which rhymes with "home") helps to purify your mind and spirit. When you vocalize it, you'll be able to feel it rumbling through you from your lower pelvis all the way to the top of your head. It can be a very powerful (and dizzying) practice. Affirmations are also repeated but aren't usually chanted like mantras. Instead, they're positive statements that help to affirm something you want to encourage in your life. For example, an affirmation I'm fond of using is "I am strong."

If none of these forms of "asking" feels right to you, then you might focus on a specific feeling that you're trying to bring more of into your life. This becomes especially useful when you aren't really sure what it is you're asking for. For example, when I was about to sell my first house, I can recall a powerful moment one night. The house was quiet and dark. I'd been slowly wandering through the rooms, saying goodbye and thinking of the transformation the house had undergone over the years. Would I ever find another home as good as this one? Eventually I found myself standing in my pajamas in the middle of the kitchen thinking about how much I'd loved living in this space. I'd thought I would live there possibly for the rest of my life, but that wasn't how things turned out. I was sad, but suddenly I was also euphorically happy.

The collision of opposing emotions was jarring, and I started crying and laughing at the same time. I was experiencing grief over the loss of my home, but at the same time I was also amazed at what I was about to receive by letting go of it. On the one hand, I had no idea what the next step held for me and I was scared I wouldn't find myself in a home like this again. On the other, I was suddenly getting a sense of all the possibilities that were just around the corner. I was overcome with a feeling that the end result was going to be even better than I could have imagined for myself.

In the end, this was exactly what happened. Living arrangements were bumpy for a while, but my next home was indeed more than I imagined I would ever be able to receive. When you don't know what you're

Affirmations are positive statements that help to affirm something you want to encourage in your life.

asking for, it's okay. Focus on the energy and emotion of where you're currently at and then how it would feel if you obtained your unknown happiness.

These forms of asking are ways you can put yourself out there and make your desires known. This is a great step in attracting the life you imagine for yourself.

Meditation (Listening and Allowing)

Now that you've put out your request, it's time to listen for the response and allow whatever is coming to you to come. In any relationship, it doesn't take long to realize the vital importance of listening. Through meditation, you're able to listen for the unicorn's response.

We already have a basic understanding of the energy body and the ability of clairvoyance, but there are other psychic skills that can help us connect with unicorn energy as well. These abilities are known as the *clairs*, and they're all useful as different forms of spiritual "listening." They can be especially helpful during meditation, so we'll dig into them in more detail in the section on psychic senses later in this chapter. After that, you'll also get a chance to try guided meditation. But first, let's look at the final thing we need to pay attention to when we're calling in the unicorn.

Mindfulness (Being Awake and Receiving)

We touched on mindfulness earlier, but we're coming back around to it here because it's such an important piece of the unicorn encounter. Remember, it doesn't do any good if you ask, prepare, and sort of listen for a unicorn encounter if you're not fully aware when it actually arrives and you don't recognize it.

This is what it looks like to be mindful on a spiritual level: You acknowledge impressions, emotions, and the subtle energetic senses. Instead of brushing away dreams, thoughts, and visions as "just" your imagination, you let them in, consider them, and allow them to speak the messages they are trying to send to you.

What does it look like to call in the unicorn? It can take so many forms, but I'll give you one example. Years ago I was on a volunteer trip for humanitarian outreach. During a bit of downtime, I was wandering around the building where we were staying and felt an urge to check out a prayer room that was tucked away. Someone had mentioned earlier that day that it was there, and it had piqued my interest. I felt silly, but I listened to my inner curiosity anyway. This was me hearing the unicorn's call. I could have brushed it away, but instead I mindfully paid attention to it and acted on it.

I eventually found the small room, and when I walked in I thought, "I don't know what I'm supposed to do." It was in part a statement to myself, but more so it was my way of asking spirit to help me out. Within my thought was also the sense that I would be guided. I felt inclined to light a candle. After I did, I noticed a few books sitting on a chair and walked over and picked them up. I was most drawn to the bottom book, a daily devotional. I opened it to that day's entry. I read the entry for that day and the next; they were both meaningful for me in the moment. One of the entries also mentioned a candle, and the synchronicity felt significant and confirming. I could feel that I was supposed to be there.

I sat down and closed my eyes. "I don't really know what to say," I prompted again, but even without knowing exactly what I was asking for, the act of opening my heart, becoming vulnerable, and seeking connection was a request in itself. Now it was time to listen.

I felt a comforting energy wash over me and relaxed into it. In my mind, I saw a spiritual figure in a field with flowers all around. When I reached him, we embraced, and the joy between us was overwhelming. I took his hand and was laughing. I could see happiness in his eyes as well. Without words, I could feel him telling me how proud he was of me. The rest I couldn't remember after the fact because I became overwhelmed and started crying, but I trusted that a part of me would retain the message if I needed it. I thanked him, and after we hugged again, I walked away. He stood there smiling, and I was still smiling too. The joy in my heart overflowed. Message received.

Becoming mindful as a practice in your daily life will help you receive what you've been asking for. Part of this will be about acknowledging occurrences by taking action, such as writing them down or taking photos in order to keep a record of all your unicorn encounters. After my experience in the prayer room, I journaled about the event as a way of solidifying my receipt of the encounter. Or you might want to share your experience with others.

A word of caution: Don't be surprised if your experience doesn't translate fully to others. If they don't come away with the same sense of awe or if you find yourself frustrated that they "just don't get it," this doesn't mean your experience wasn't meaningful and true. I could explain my prayer-room moment a million times over, but no one other than me will ever feel the full impact of it.

chapter six

Making a spiritual connection and receiving a message can be very powerful, but these moments can be hard to describe and words usually don't do them justice. Fully comprehending the magic of these moments is based in personal authentic immersion in the energy and emotion of the experience. Still, if you're inspired to share with others, go for it. Just know that it's equally valid to hold your experience as a private blessing to cherish alone.

Psychic Senses as Tools for Listening

There's a bit of a trick to listening for your unicorn's call. Knowing this will help you pay more mindful attention as well. In the same way that there are unicorn tools that help us receive and pay attention to the unicorn's call, there are also tools that help us *listen* for it. These are our intuitive and energetic senses and abilities.

We traditionally consider that we have five basic senses: sight, hearing, touch, taste, and smell. But we actually have more senses than

> When you are mindful on a spiritual level, you acknowledge impressions, emotions, and the subtle energetic senses.

this. Some of these include a sense of spacial awareness, pain, balance, temperature, or acceleration, and the perception of time or the feeling that something is familiar. Some people even perceive senses in entirely different ways. For example, they might see sounds in the form of color or experience some sight as smell.

In addition to these traditional and nontraditional senses are our energetic senses. These are known as the *clairs*, because the terms all begin with *clair*, which means "clear." These senses connect us to our intuitive guidance. Even if you weren't aware of them previously, you've certainly been using them. Let's take a closer look at the clairs.

Clairvoyance (Sight)

Clairvoyance is the ability to visually perceive energetic messages through your psychic vision. These messages usually appear within your inner vision in the mind's eye and are not perceived with your physical eyes, although some people do perceive psychic imagery that way as well.

To get an idea of how clairvoyance works, picture your bedroom. Now see your bed and envision the pattern on your blanket or bedspread. The way you're internally seeing the images and details of the space is the same way that we see with clairvoyance. This ability is very useful during meditation and energy work.

Clairaudience (Sound)

Clairaudience is the ability to perceive energetic messages through the inner ear. By "inner ear," I don't mean the internal structure of the physical ear. Instead, this is the ear's version of our inner vision/mind's eye. When you get a song stuck in your head, you're using the inner ear that I'm referring to. For some people though, clairaudience can come across as sounding the same as their normal physical hearing. Most often we'll psychically hear in a way that's internal, and on rare occasions it will come across as external noise or communication, such as a loud noise or your name being called.

Usually clairaudience ends up sounding a lot like your own internal thoughts. Because of this, it can take time before you're able to clearly perceive the difference between clairaudient communication and your own thoughts. With practice, it becomes much more obvious. Like a fingerprint, we all have a distinct voice and energy. When communication is coming from a source other than you, it feels different, but this is a subtlety that can take time to distinguish.

Claircognizance (Knowing)

Claircognizance is an energetic sense of knowing. It's when you know something down to your core even when you aren't sure why. There is just no logical reason for how you know the information.

This used to happen with Amy and me all the time. It seemed like whenever either of us called the other, the receiver always knew who was calling without even looking at the ID. This never happened for me with anyone else and our calls were very random, so there was no pattern or reason to support our knowing. It was simply a connection and energetic communication that left us certain of who was on the other end.

Clairsentience (Feeling)

Clairsentience is the ability to perceive energetic messages of sensation or feeling. This is the gut instinct that we often hear about. You might feel pushed in a certain direction but don't quite know why. Or perhaps you've just met someone and you get the sense that there's danger or mischief about them. Without words, you're reading spaces, people, events, and situations to feel out information that's helpful for you to know.

chapter six

217

If you perform psychic readings or energy therapies like Reiki or Healing Touch, this ability allows you to feel specific messages and energies that you're working with. When you're giving someone a massage, you might feel a stabbing pain in your head if they get frequent migraines that need attending to on an energetic level. In a psychic reading, the medium might feel tightness in their chest while connecting with someone who passed away from a heart attack.

Clairsentience has spin-offs that can be further defined. These include clairempathy, clairolfaction, clairgustance, and clairtangency. These are all specific types of psychic feeling.

Clairempathy (Emotion)

Clairempathy is the ability to energetically feel another's emotional experience. It's a form of clairsentience but is specific to emotion. People who are strongly aligned with this ability are known as *empaths*. It's very common for these individuals to confuse these energetic connections and messages as being their own. Because of this, they might go through their day taking on a teacher's anger, a friend's distress, a cashier's depression, and more. While positive feelings can be felt as well, negativity is something that empaths unknowingly tend to soak up like a sponge and struggle with, which is why clairempathy can be an exhausting ability.

Unconsciously, we as empaths want to heal and help resolve other people's pain, but we need to tend to our needs first. If you feel down, anxious, burnt-out, or overwhelmed, make it a regular practice to ask yourself, "Where is this feeling coming from? Is it mine? Or is it someone else's?" Listen to the internal answers that come to you. If the feeling is yours, try to identify its origins so you can work through it. If it *isn't* yours, ask spirit to help you release the energy back to the owner so they can heal and resolve it. You could even try Exercise 17: Unicorn Chakra Energy Clearing, which we did at the end of chapter 5. Afterward, ground yourself by engaging in a physical activity. Go for a run, dance around the house, or stomp your feet. This pulls your own energy back into your body. Empathy is a wonderful ability, but it is one that demands a lot of self-care and awareness.

Clairolfaction (Smell) and Clairgustance (Taste)

Clairolfaction (also known as clairalience) is the ability to perceive energetic messages through your psychic sense of smell. The smell is perceived without the assistance of your physical nose, since the scent isn't actually coming from anything in your physical environment. Clairgustance is the ability to perceive energetic messages through your psychic sense of taste when you're not actually eating anything.

These two senses often work together, since our physical experience of them often happens in unison. Perhaps your grandfather always chewed spearmint gum, and the taste and smell of it comes to you when he wants you to know he's near.

Clairtangency (Touch)

Clairtangency is also known as psychometry. This is the ability to receive energetic information through touch. Some mediums use this ability during readings by holding an object that belonged to the person they're trying to communicate with. In doing so, they're able to gather information about the history of the object in their hands and the person connected with it.

★ ★ ★

We don't have to be skilled in all of these psychic abilities. As with left- or right-handedness, we're usually stronger in one ability or a certain number of them rather than all of them. But we do use all of these abilities to a certain degree. Clairaudience, clairvoyance, clairsentience, claircognizance, and clairempathy are usually the most prominent senses. Being aware of them during your meditation practice can take your experience to a whole new level.

• EXERCISE 18 •
Your Strong Senses

In this meditation, you'll get the chance to make use of the psychic senses that we just covered to see which ones are most natural to you. Find a comfortable spot where you won't be disturbed. In your mind's eye, find yourself back in the favorite meditation space that you first explored in chapter 4 in Exercise 13: Learning to Trust Your Inner Wisdom. As you reemerge in this space, pay attention to the details that first come to you. The sights and sounds of an environment are typically what we notice first, but maybe for you it's a feeling or an emotion that's most immediately noticeable. Tune into whatever those details are, and see if they lead you anywhere or have more to say.

Once you've absorbed those details, see your unicorn heading toward you from the edge of the space. Soon enough, they're standing in front of you. As a blessing to each other, you touch your hand to their heart and feel them energetically reach out to your heart as well. You both bow your heads until your foreheads touch and their alicorn rests atop your crown. A light forms around you both, uniting the two of you in a single shimmering orb. Take a moment to feel the energy moving through you.

Soon the light fades and you take a step back from each other. Your unicorn wants to share a message with you, and you stand facing them, ready to receive it. Allow the information to come to you. You might be shown something as a vision, or you might hear the message directly as a thought. You might suddenly know something that you didn't realize before, or you might feel the sharing of a sensation or an emotion. Be open to however the message comes to you, and know that it might come to you through more than one of your psychic senses. When you've received your message, show thanks to your unicorn in whatever way you prefer and slowly come back to your physical space.

The intuitive senses that you experience most prominently in this practice (and any of the other meditative and energetic practices throughout the book) are indicative of those you naturally prefer. The more you work with them, the more easily you'll notice them as you go about your days.

Unicorns Do Not Walk Alone

So far you've had numerous opportunities to meet and connect with your unicorn guides using the practices throughout this book. Maybe you've had no trouble making these connections and your unicorns have appeared with ease. If so, that's wonderful! If that hasn't been your experience, don't be disheartened. This new bit of information I'm about to share may be just the tip you've been waiting for.

When I started actively trying to reconnect with my unicorn guide, I was first met by Michael, one of my most prominent spirit guides. He has a presence that feels larger than life and connects very strongly with my heart energy. This could easily come across as overwhelming, but he tempers it with a sense of silliness that brings him down to earth, so to speak. When Michael appeared in my mind's eye during a medita-tion, I could see my unicorn just behind him, with the physical size and broadness of a Clydes-dale horse. The unicorn was mostly white, but from its upper back and down to its tail

there were irregular patches of brown flecked with gold. Visual details were coming through to me, but I felt a lack of connection to this being.

Annoyed and confused, I repeatedly tried to sidestep Michael, yet even though the unicorn towered over him, it always remained at his back. When I tried to connect energetically with the unicorn, I felt a calm silence and strength. I listened for anything it had to say but heard nothing. Michael laughed, knowing my frustration, but just observed me as I felt things out for myself.

I tuned into both of their energies and saw Michael's close connection to my heart chakra, while the unicorn connected to me more broadly and at a bit of a distance. The energy spread like wings around the outer ring of my aura, far from my physical body. I sensed that unicorn energy takes a broad role in how it influences us and our lives. Their connection is like a slow and steady sprinkle of rain that filters in subtly through all the layers of our energy body, hitting wherever it's needed. Instead of supporting a specific purpose or fine-tuning the small day-to-day details of our lives, they step back and allow their energy to trickle in to impact our lives in a gentle yet powerful way.

I found this new information fascinating, and I learned soon after that my understanding of unicorn energy aligns with that of author and energy worker Cordelia Francesca Brabbs, who says, "Unicorns love to help out with bigger-picture, soul-purpose issues in our lives" (Brabbs 2018, 9). She goes on to explain that simple daily guidance, like finding a great parking spot, is handled by our other guides, but unicorns do well with the things that move us toward our soul purpose. "They want to see you shining your light, loving yourself, living from your magic and being a powerful force for good in this world."

Back in my meditation, I finally asked Michael, "Why are you here?"

"I'm a bridge to your unicorn," he replied.

Immediately, I thought of how people guide animals on leashes and reins, but that analogy felt off. It isn't that unicorns need to be led or contained. It's simply that their energy is so heightened and expansive that having a guide you're already connected with helps to filter and translate the message that your unicorn is trying to communicate to you.

I was surprised to learn that the unicorn may be silent and come with another guide who communicates on their behalf. This makes sense though. Unicorns are of such a high vibration that we can have a hard time translating their communications. It's not that they don't want to speak with us directly or that they think they're "too good" to be in direct contact with us. It's just a matter of differing energetic frequencies. Think of it like a radio or the high-pitched whistles used with dogs. If we don't have the capability to tune into the unicorn's high frequency, we might miss out. To help things, another guide that we're very connected with (consciously or not) may act as a bridge to sync us up with the unicorn's high vibration.

• EXERCISE 19 •
Meet Your Bridging Guide

As you did in the previous exercise, envision being in your favorite meditation space. Connect to the sounds, sights, feelings, and energy of that space. Enjoy it for a moment. Now see your unicorn walking toward you from the edge of your location, but this time they're being led by your bridging guide. It's possible and even likely that this guide is someone you're already familiar with.

Pay attention to the details of the guide's appearance: what they're wearing; whether their hair is long, free-flowing, or tied up in a knot; if they're barefoot or wearing footwear; or if they have any tattoos or jewelry adornments that hint at who they are or what they represent to you. Paying attention to the details helps to strengthen your intuitive abilities.

Once the guide is in front of you, greet them in whatever way feels natural. Maybe you're bursting with excitement and want to give them a hug. Or if you're feeling reserved and a bit overwhelmed, you might give a simple bow.

After your greeting, you take a step back and your bridging guide reaches their hand out to you. They place it on the crown of your head. See, listen, and feel for any insights that come to you as your crown chakra lights up with their touch. They remove their hand and touch their fingertips to your forehead. As your third eye lights up, tune into any insights that come to you. Next they remove their hand and place their fingertips at the center of your chest over your heart chakra, which starts to glow. Once again, pay attention to any information that you receive.

Your bridging guide now gently places their hands on your shoulders and looks into your eyes. They want to share your unicorn's message. Receive the message they have for you in whatever form it takes. Once you're done, thank them both in whatever way feels right to you and slowly come back to your physical space. Take time to process and record your experience.

The Unicorn's True Meaning

Finally, we come to the end and the true meaning of the unicorn: realizing our divinity. On the surface, unicorns seem to be about the search for the individual. They're rare and they appear as single isolated creatures. It's easy to assume that they represent finding what's unique about the individual, the isolated "one." But that's the illusion. Their role is actually larger than that. The unicorn is truly about the search for our own inner divinity and the light that connects us to one another as "One."

I feel this sentiment when Tess Whitehurst says in her book *Unicorn Magic*, "You are stardust, briefly masquerading as a physical being. On the other hand, you are a precious creature, animated with infinite wisdom, glowing and sparkling with the same energy that gave birth to the cosmos" (Whitehurst 2019, chap. 2). We are individuals, but not, because in the end we're all made from the same amazing, mysterious, and wonderful star-stuff.

Have you ever felt a "remembering" of this unity? It can be a gentle sense of loving connection or an overwhelming feeling that takes you over completely. I've experienced this at concerts where the energies of the individuals in the band and the audience expand and merge into one united and happy whole. I've felt it during emergencies when random people come together to help someone they don't even know. I've even sensed it while driving, when I'm traveling alongside the same cars for a while and eventually one splits off from the group, and it feels as though I've parted with a teammate (the polar opposite of road rage).

With this feeling of unity, there's always an underlying energy of love and an opening of the heart. Strangers feel like loved friends and family; it doesn't matter that we don't know them. Energy is energy. Spirit is spirit. We feel that we're all the same and connected to one another through a universal uniting force. We're trying to experience, identify, and imagine the divine. Unicorns are just one form of that experience.

• EXERCISE 20 •
Defining Your Unicorn

We often have a descriptor or label that helps define our personal spiritual experience. This can indicate where we find inspiration and guidance. For some, their label for this higher wisdom is *God* or *Goddess*, and for others it's *the divine*. You might find comfort with angels and guardians. Maybe you find connection with a specific deity, saint, or spirit guide. Perhaps there is a certain religious figure or higher power that you connect most strongly to. Or you might take a broader perspective and call it *universal energy* or simply *spirit*. Or your label could be something more tangible, like *nature* or *music*. Or, just maybe, you call it *unicorn*.

Whatever form this spiritual energy takes for us and no matter what label we use for it, the thing we're all seeking is the same: the experience of divine love. As with our unicorn people, the outer heroes or labels that we find comfort and inspiration in usually end up offering a reflection of ourselves in some way. The form isn't the important thing. The significant piece is the feeling and experience of love and joy that we find there,

An experience of authentic divine love can be an incredible reminder of our inner light and the connection we have to one another.

along with a clearer understanding of ourselves. Like my meditation in the prayer room, an experience of authentic divine love can be an incredible reminder of our inner light and the connection we have to one another through a uniting energy.

• EXERCISE 21 •
Calling In the Unicorn

If you've been able to clearly define your label for spiritual energy or higher wisdom, try calling in the unicorn specific to your spiritual descriptor. Remember the steps of ritual, prayer, mantra, and affirmation (asking and attracting); meditation (listening and allowing); and mindfulness (being awake and receiving). Also remember the psychic tools and see which ones rise to the surface as being most useful to you.

In ritual, you create space by choosing a place dedicated to your purposeful event at a time when you won't be distracted. Choose a location and make it a meaningful and inviting place. For me, this translates to a sunny and cozy room full of plants, crystals, and a collection of creative things.

Set an intention that indicates the purpose of your request. If you aren't sure what that purpose is, or you have an idea but aren't positive of the outcome you're looking for, find the emotion and feeling attached to it. Focus on intention instead of anticipation. Intention is something that you hope and intend will happen. But instead of greedily saying, "This is what I want, now give it to me," with intention you're respectfully saying, "This is what I desire. Please show me how to align myself with it so that I may receive it."

Build energy and put out the request. Say it, write it, express it. This might mean you journal or sing the words of your intention. Or while thinking of your intention and where it may lead, you might feel and express emotion that comes from it through tears or laughter. Or you could take certain actions that plant seeds leading toward your end goal. There are innumerable ways to express your request.

Let go of your intention with a thankful heart. Don't obsess over your request, but be watchful of ways you are being asked to align with your intention. Try to let go of expectations and instead focus on gratitude for being heard and the things you're already experiencing that align with your intention.

Set a meditation schedule, whether it's once a day or once a week. Take this time to stop, listen, and allow.

Find ways that will remind you to be mindful throughout your days to make sure you're awake and receiving. Acknowledge impressions, emotions, and the subtle energetic senses. Instead of brushing away dreams, thoughts, and visions as "just" your imagination, let them in, consider them, and allow them to speak the messages they're trying to send to you.

★ ★ ★

Calling in the unicorn is a lifetime practice. There are exercises and actions we can take to strengthen our muscles of awareness, some of which can be found right in this chapter. But beyond that, we are always evolving and finding the tools and practices that work most effectively for us. Maybe for you it's joining a coaching group that lights you up and brings you the joy you've been unable to find on your own because it brings a sense of community, support, and inspiration. Or maybe you're the opposite and you need to create a private sanctuary where you can embrace more of these individual and spiritual exercises independently in order to connect more strongly with yourself and the divine energy that exists within you.

Whatever it looks like for you, the unicorn is there within you. Go out (or within) and find it. The sparkle is waiting for you to cast a light on it and really make it shine.

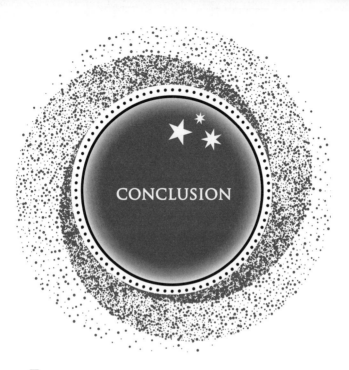

CONCLUSION

I'm so grateful that you've come here to learn all about unicorns with me. I hope you'll carry what you've learned into your daily life for inspiration. Pay attention to your dreams and any moments of synchronicity. Listen to the beauty that catches you. When you see a rose that stops you in your tracks, take a moment to bend down and smell it. If you hear a beat that gets your toes tapping, follow it.

Always remember that the most effective way to raise your vibration isn't through finding the perfect stone or practicing self-care in a glitzy, social-media-worthy way. There isn't a single answer or quick fix to attaining constant joy or permanent health. These states of being eventually falter, but it's not superficial impermanence that we've been seeking here anyway. Instead, attaining true balance and happiness has more to do with reawakening a sense of wonder and finding the ways that this awakened awe arises for you.

This sense of wonder is running like glitter deep in your veins, and you become more aware of it through the way you experience your day-to-day life. Be curious. Feed your passions and let your authentic self emerge. Find your unicorns and be one for someone else. The world needs you for all the goodness and glitter that you are, so for your sake and everyone else's, shine on!

BIBLIOGRAPHY

Alexander, Skye. *Unicorns: The Myths, Legends, and Lore.* Avon, MA: Simon & Schuster, 2015.

Alvarez, Melissa. *Animal Frequency: Identify, Attune, and Connect to the Energy of Animals.* Woodbury, MN: Llewellyn, 2017.

American Museum of Natural History. "Unicorns, West and East." Accessed March 3, 2019. https://www.amnh.org/exhibitions/mythic-creatures/land-creatures-of-the-earth/unicorns-west-and-east.

Animal Planet. "Mythical Animals That Turned Out to Be Real." Accessed March 3, 2019. http://www.animalplanet.com/tv -shows/monster-week/mythical-animals-that-turned-out -to-be-real/.

Beagle, Peter S. Adaptation by Peter B. Gillis. *The Last Unicorn*. San Diego, CA: IDW Publishing, 2011.

Brabbs, Cordelia Francesca. *Oracle of the Unicorns*. Victoria, Australia: Blue Angel Publishing, 2018.

Gonzales, Dave. "10 Magical Facts about Unicorns." Mental Floss. June 27, 2013. http://mentalfloss.com/article/51424/10 -magical-facts-about-unicorns.

Higley, Connie, and Alan Higley. *Reference Guide for Essential Oils*. Spanish Fork, UT: Abundant Health, 2012.

Hudson Institute of Mineralogy. Mindat.org. https://www.mindat.org.

Kosintsev, Pavel, Kieren J. Mitchell, Thibaut Devièse et al. "Evolution and Extinction of the Giant Rhinoceros *Elasmotherium Sibiricum* Sheds Light on Late Quaternary Megafaunal Extinctions." *Nature Ecology & Evolution* 3 (January 2019): 31–38. https:// doi.org/10.1038/s41559-018-0722-0.

Kynes, Sandra. *Crystal Magic*. Woodbury, MN: Llewellyn, 2017.

LaGravenese, Richard, and Steven Rogers. *P.S. I Love You*. Based on the 2004 novel of the same name by Cecelia Ahern. Directed by Richard LaGravenese. Warner Bros. Pictures, 2007.

Lembo, Margaret Ann. *Crystals Beyond Beginners: Awaken Your Consciousness with Precious Gifts from the Earth*. Woodbury, MN: Llewellyn, 2019.

———. *The Essential Guide to Crystals, Minerals, and Stones*. Woodbury, MN: Llewellyn, 2013.

LeVan, Angie. "Seeing Is Believing: The Power of Visualization." *Psychology Today*, Dec. 3, 2009. https://www.psychologytoday .com/intl/blog/flourish/200912/seeing-is-believing-the-power -visualization.

McAllister, Murray J., PsyD. Leader of group discussion at Courage Kenny Rehabilitation Institute, Stillwater, MN, August 24, 2018.

Mosin, Oleg, and Ignat Ignatov. "The Structure and Composition of Natural Carbonaceous Fullerene Containing Mineral Shungite." *International Journal of Advanced Scientific and Technical Research* 6, no. 3 (Nov.–Dec. 2013). https://www.rspublication.com/ijst/dec13/2.pdf.

Nichols, Andrew. "The Complete Fragments of Ctesias of Cnidus: Translation and Commentary with an Introduction." PhD diss., University of Florida, 2008. http://etd.fcla.edu/UF/UFE0022 521/nichols_a.pdf.

Rowling, J. K. *Harry Potter and the Deathly Hallows.* New York: Arthur A. Levine Books, 2007.

Sajo, Ma Easter Joy, Cheol-Su Kim, Soo-Ki Kim, Kwang Yong Shim, Tae-Young Kang, and Kyu-Jae Lee. "Antioxidant and Anti-Inflammatory Effects of Shungite against Ultraviolet B Irradiation-Induced Skin Damage in Hairless Mice." *Oxidative Medicine and Cellular Longevity*, vol. 2017, Article ID 7340143, 11 pages, 2017. https://doi.org/10.1155/2017/7340143.

University of the Arts. "Young Woman Seated in a Landscape with a Unicorn." Universal Leonardo. Accessed March 3, 2019. http://www.universalleonardo.org/work.php?id=438.

Whitehurst, Tess. *Unicorn Magic: Awaken to Mystical Energy to Embrace Your Personal Power.* Woodbury, MN: Llewellyn, 2019.

RECOMMENDED
RESOURCES

To purchase a unicorn energy mist kit, receive free coloring pages, and participate in an online class based on the practices in this book, visit www.AngelaAnn.Wix .com/arts.

The following are additional materials that I love and recommend for your own insight, inspiration, and fun. Sources that I've cited throughout the book also fit here, so make sure to refer to the bibliography as well.

Unicorns

Lawson, Jenny. "Unicorn Success Club." The Bloggess.
   http://thebloggess.com/2012/03/07/unicorn-success-club/.

Loehr, Mallory C. *I'm a Unicorn*. New York: Golden Books, 2018.

Simpson, Dana. *Phoebe and Her Unicorn*. Kansas City, MO: Andrews
   McMeel Publishing, 2014.

Taylor, Joules. *The Wisdom of Unicorns*. New York: Clarkson Potter,
   2017.

Authenticity

Dillard, Sherrie. *Discover Your Authentic Self: Be You, Be Free,
   Be Happy*. Woodbury, MN: Llewellyn, 2016.

Lawson, Jenny. *Furiously Happy: A Funny Book About Horrible Things*.
   New York: Flatiron Books, 2015.

Markul, Tanya. *Thug Unicorn*. http://thugunicorn.com.

Mathews, Andrea. *Letting Go of Good: Dispel the Myth of Goodness to
   Find Your Genuine Self*. Woodbury, MN: Llewellyn, 2017.

Sincero, Jen. *You Are a Badass: How to Stop Doubting Your Greatness
   and Start Living an Awesome Life*. Philadelphia, PA: Running
   Press, 2016.

Decluttering

Kondo, Marie. *The Life-Changing Magic of Tidying Up: The Japanese
   Art of Decluttering and Organizing*. Berkeley, CA: Ten Speed
   Press, 2014.

MacLeod, Janice. *Paris Letters: One Woman's Journey from the Fast
   Lane to a Slow Stroll in Paris*. Naperville, IL: Sourcebooks, 2014.

Morris, Tisha. *Clutter Intervention: How Your Stuff Is Keeping You
   Stuck*. Woodbury, MN: Llewellyn, 2018.

Essential Oils

Higley, Connie, and Alan Higley. *Reference Guide for Essential Oils.* Spanish Fork, UT: Abundant Health, 2012.

National Association for Holistic Aromatherapy. "Safety Information." https://naha.org/index.php/explore-aromatherapy/safety/.

recommended resources

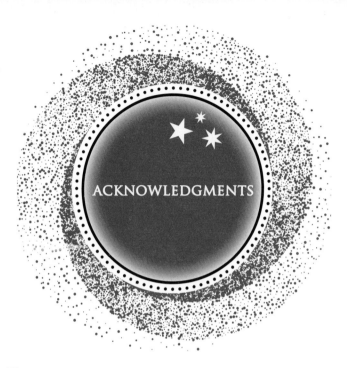

ACKNOWLEDGMENTS

I'm honored for the assistance I've received in this endeavor. First, thank you to all the players at Llewellyn (so many more than I can name here) who supported this lifelong dream in becoming a reality. Your enthusiasm, partially demonstrated by all the unicorns that now sporadically appear in my workspace, is a true inspiration.

In addition, many thanks are extended:

To Amy Glaser, Andrea Neff, Terry Lohmann, and Elysia Gallo for your extra eyes and feedback. Your time and support brought me the gift of confidence.

To Shira Atakpu, who somehow channeled my ten-year-old self to create the fantastic design elements in the book. And to Donna Burch-Brown for applying her magic touch to get it all in just the right place.

To Echo Bodine, Melissa Alvarez, and Murray McAllister for allowing me to share bits of your wisdom within these pages. I'm glad you're a part of it.

To Meghan Kane for your support through my processing of life experience. Your insight and guidance have made me, and this book, better for it. I am forever grateful.

To my family and friends for being my cheerleaders along the way.

To Lucas Wix for accommodating my odd interests and giving me the space to disappear into myself for a while, and for always reminding me to eventually come back out into the world. You are my #1 unicorn.

To the muses in spirit who guided me through all the hours of writing.

And above all, to you, fellow unicorn-tribe member. You are the purpose! Without you I would be writing to myself. I appreciate your search and am deeply honored to have had the chance to connect with you.